BIBLE FOUNDATIONS
New Testament Overview

STUDENT WORKBOOK

PATRICIA C. RUSSELL

EDITOR
MRS. NELLIE E. CONSTANCE

GRAPHIC DESIGN
TROY D. RUSSELL

PROJECT EDITOR
TOM M. CONSTANCE JR.

EXPLORER'S BIBLE STUDY

P. O. BOX 425
DICKSON, TN 37056-0425

We believe the Bible is God's Word, a divine revelation, in the original language verbally inspired in its entirety, and that it is the supreme infallible authority in all matters of faith and conduct.
(II Peter 1:21; II Timothy 3:16).

Printed in the United States of America

Published by Explorer's Bible Study
2652 Hwy. 46 South
P.O. Box 425
Dickson, TN 37056-0425

Contents

About the Author

Pat Russell has been a Christian educator for over 25 years. She began her teaching career by forming a pre-school in her home. Later she accepted a position as a teacher in a private Christian School and also served as a curriculum coordinator and consultant. Most recently, she helped to co-found Carden Christian Academy in Park City, Utah. Through years of writing and development, she has crafted a curriculum that comes from practical "hands on" experience. This curriculum has been "classroom tested" in Christian Schools, in Home School settings, as well as having been used in Explorer's Bible Study classes throughout the U.S.

Pat's goal in developing this curriculum is to provide the young Bible scholar with a chronological and historical method of Bible study. It is through this means that the Bible is seen in its entirety, not in broken pieces. The importance of understanding the true meaning of God's Word and His plan for each of us comes through careful study. Interpretation follows a knowledge of what God says, what God means, and finally how each individual applies this knowledge to his or her personal life experience.

A Note to Parents and Teachers

If you have said 'yes' to the call of God to teach, you have accepted one of the most important challenges in building the future kingdom. In James 3:1 we read "Not many should become teachers, knowing that there will be a stricter Judgment." It takes a great commitment to put ourselves in a place of responsibility in which children and young students will make life-changing decisions based on the life and teaching we put before them. But knowing the high expectations God has for those who commit to this calling should not deter one from this wonderful and powerful opportunity to serve in this way. As you see the loving response to God from a child or student, it is difficult - if not impossible - to imagine NOT teaching! It becomes a compelling urgency that God rewards in so many ways that you'll wonder why there was ever a question mark after the words, "Should I consider teaching?"

Whether you are a home schooling parent, a Sunday School teacher, or a Christian educator, God has chosen you to teach! As a teacher, you will have a great influence in the lives of your children or students. You have been given the responsibility by God to mentor these lives spiritually. It is an awesome responsibility but you don't have to do it alone! God is with you every step of the way.

Teach each child faithfully, prayerfully and consistently in His Word......Knowing it, Believing it, Living it and then Teaching it. Teaching is impossible without the first three. We hope this Bible curriculum will help guide you through this process.

A guide for those who are called to teach. A Teacher must have:

1. A personal commitment to Christ.

2. A love for students with a desire to see them understand the Word of God.

3. A call to the ministry through God's Word .

4. A personal commitment to daily Bible study and to complete the lesson each week.

"And these words which I command you today shall be in your heart. You shall teach them diligently to your children, and shall talk of them when you sit in your house, when you walk by the way, when you lie down, and when you rise up."
Deuteronomy 6:6 -7

A Note to the Student - How to Use this Workbook

The lessons in this workbook will help you learn more about God and to better understand His Word - the Bible.

Each lesson has a **Bible Story** for you to read that will help you know more about God's Word. Read the story slowly and carefully. If there are words you don't know, look it up in a dictionary or ask someone who can help you.

Guided Prayer Thoughts will help you as you talk to God.

Bible Words to Remember will help you as you memorize and remember verses from the Bible.

Use your dictionary to look up **Word Meanings** for your lesson.

The **Questions** will help you to think about and remember the Bible story you have read. I think you will find that the questions are fun to do!

You may want to get an art notebook and make a drawing for each lesson you study!

As you study......

1. Pray that God will give you understanding.

2. Find out what the Bible says.

3. Choose to live God's way every day.

5. Never stop learning and growing...there is always MORE!

BIBLE STORY

Mary was a young woman who lived in the small town of Nazareth. She was in love with a man named Joseph who was a carpenter. They planned to get married soon. As she was quietly thinking, she was suddenly surprised when a voice said, REJOICE! It was a beautiful sound but Mary wondered what it meant. She looked up and saw an angel who told her the most wonderful news: Mary, you are favored by God. Do not be afraid because God is with you. He has chosen you to be the mother of God's own Son. You will name Him JESUS. He will be great and will be called the Son of the Highest. He will reign as King and His kingdom will have no end."

Mary was amazed at this marvelous announcement. She and her people had waited for a very long time for God's promise of a Savior. She believed that God's promises were true, but could she really be the chosen one to be the mother of this special baby? Mary said to the angel, "I am not yet married to Joseph. How is it possible that I would have a child?" The angel answered, "This baby will come by the power of God through the Holy Spirit. Nothing is impossible with God."

Mary was filled with joy as she listened and believed what the angel had told her and said, "I am the Lord's handmaiden. Let it happen just as you have said."

Then the angel of the Lord appeared to Joseph in a dream. The angel gave him the message about Mary being the mother of God's Son. The angel told him to not be worried about taking Mary as his wife because the baby she would have would save all people from their sins if they believed in Him. Joseph believed the angel's message.

Mary and Joseph were soon married. They were very happy and knew that God would take care of them. When the Roman ruler commanded all the people to go back to the city in which they were born to be counted, Mary and Joseph began their journey to Bethlehem which was about eighty miles from Nazareth. It was in this city that Jesus, God's Son would be born.

God was watching over them and even though there were no rooms left for them to stay in the Inn when they arrived in the city of Bethlehem, there was a warm stable where they could rest. It was on this very special night that God sent His Son to come to the world to bring His love to all people.

GUIDED PRAYER THOUGHTS

Thank you God for sending Your very own Son Jesus to show us what Your love is really like! Help us to share this Good News with others.

BIBLE WORDS TO REMEMBER

He will be great and will be called the Son of the Highest...and of His kingdom there will be no end.

Luke 1:32-33

WORD MEANINGS

messenger: _____

rejoice: _____

meant: _____

favored: _____

reign: _____

kingdom: _____

handmaiden: _____

journey: _____

Inn: _____

QUESTIONS

1. **Tell three things about Mary:**

   a. _____

   b. _____

   c. _____

2. **Who did God choose to be the mother of His own Son?** _____

   _____

3. **What four things did the angel tell her?**

   a. _____

   b. _____

   c. _____

   d. _____

4. **What else would God's Son be called?**_____

   _____

5. **Complete: He will_____as king and His _____**

   will have no_____.

6. What question did she ask the angel? _____

    _____

7. Complete: The angel said, "Nothing is _____
    with _____.

8. Tell the message of God the angel gave to Joseph in a dream?

    _____

    _____

9. What would be the purpose of this very special baby? _____

    _____

    _____

10. Which city did Mary and Joseph travel to? _____

11. How far was Bethlehem from Nazareth? _____

    _____

12. Why did they have to make this journey?_____

    _____

    _____

13. Give the reason that Mary and Joseph stayed in the stable.

    _____

14. Who was watching and taking care of Mary and Joseph?

    _____

    _____

15. What would Jesus show to all the world? _____

    _____

BIBLE STORY

On the night that Jesus was born in Bethlehem, there were shepherds in the fields nearby watching their sheep. It was a quiet night until suddenly, they heard angels singing. The sky was bright just like it was in the daytime. It was God's glory in the heavens! The shepherds were frightened and fell to the ground, covering their eyes from the brightness.

An angel spoke to them and said, "Do not be afraid; for I am bringing you news of great joy, which shall be for all people; There is a baby that was born this day in Bethlehem, the city of David, who is the Savior, Christ the Lord."

Then the angel told the shepherds where they could find the baby so that they could go and worship Him. The shepherds looked up and saw that the sky was filled with many angels singing, "Glory to God in the highest....and on earth peace, goodwill to all men!"

When the angels disappeared, the shepherds hurried to the place where Jesus was and knelt down and worshiped Him.

Far away in another land to the east of Bethlehem were some other men who were very wise and studied the stars. They had been looking for a special star that would tell the birth of the baby that God had promised.

On the night that Jesus was born, this wonderful star appeared in the sky and the men knew what this meant--that the great king had been born in the world. They decided to follow the star and go to worship this king.

It was a long and difficult journey. They kept searching the sky and continued to follow that one magnificent star. And finally they came to the place where Jesus was. The wise men knelt down and worshiped Him. They gave Him their treasures; special gifts that were meant for a king---the

King who would save all people and show the world God's love in a way that everyone could understand.

GUIDED PRAYER THOUGHTS

> *We are thankful for the best gift of all which is Your Son, Jesus. Help us to show Your love to others because of Your great love for us.*

BIBLE WORDS TO REMEMBER

> *Glory to God in the highest, And on earth peace, goodwill toward men!*
>
> Matthew 2:14

WORD MEANINGS

glory: _____

savior: _____

worship: _____

shepherds: _____

peace: _____

goodwill: _____

knelt: _____

appeared: _____

follow: _____

difficult: _____

searching: _____

continue: _____

magnificent: _____

finally: _____

treasures: _____

_____

QUESTIONS

1. Who was in the fields on the night Jesus was born? _____

2. What were they doing? _____
_____

3. Who surprised and frightened them?
_____

4. What news was given to them? _____
_____

5. Where did this event take place? _____
_____

6. What did the shepherds do after they heard the news? _____
_____

7. Who else knew that a king had been born?
_____
_____

8. How did they know? _____
_____

9. How did they find the place where Jesus was? _____
_____

10. What two things did they do when they found Jesus?

     a. _____

     b. _____

11. Why was Jesus a special baby? _____

_____

12. Why did God send Jesus? _____

_____

BIBLE STORY

While Jesus was growing to be a man He studied and learned about God. Mary and Joseph prayed for Him and took Him to the temple where He talked with men who were very wise. But what surprised the wise men at the temple, His parents, and all those who knew Him, was that He knew the answers to all the questions and He could teach them the things about God that they did not understand.

Jesus never did anything wrong. He was kind to everyone. He never disobeyed His parents or teachers. He loved people everywhere. He was absolutely perfect because He was God's own Son----the only ONE who had ever been or would be on earth that never sinned. Jesus talked often with His Heavenly Father so that He would know the right time to do the work that God had sent Him to do.

While Jesus was waiting for God to tell Him the perfect time to start His mission on earth, another man named John was telling people what they must do to be ready for Jesus. "You must repent of your sins." Some people who listened to John thought that because they went to church and did good deeds they did not need to say they were sorry for their sins. They said, "I'm a good person."

Other people asked John what they should do because they knew they had not pleased God and were doing wrong things. So John told them that God wanted them to care for others by not taking money from them and to share what they had with the poor.

Then John, who was also called 'the baptist' told them that they should go into the water and be baptized to show that they were sorry for their sins so that they could be clean before God. He stood by the Jordon River and many people were baptized. This would show to everyone that they wanted to live a better life that would be pleasing to God.

As John was telling the people that Jesus would be coming to be a sacrifice for the sins of people, he looked up and there was Jesus! He was walking toward the water and John. John said to everyone there, "Here He comes!" John knew that Jesus was the Son of God.

Jesus had come to be baptized by John even though he had never sinned. John did not understand and did not feel worthy to baptize Jesus. But Jesus knew it was God's will to do this to show the people that He was from God.

After Jesus was baptized, a wonderful thing happened-- the sky separated and a beautiful dove which was the sign of the Holy Spirit came to Jesus. Then all the people heard the voice of God from heaven: "This is My beloved Son, in whom I am well pleased."

**GUIDED
PRAYER
THOUGHTS**

*Dear God, Thank you for Jesus. Help us
to prepare our hearts so that we will see His
salvation and accept Your gift of love.*

BIBLE WORDS TO REMEMBER

Prepare the way of the Lord
Make His paths straight.

Matthew 3:4

WORD MEANINGS

temple: _____

wise: _____

_____

mission: _____

sins: _____

repent: _____

_____

baptized: _____

_____

sacrifice: _____

_____

worthy: _____

beloved: _____

pleased: _____

QUESTIONS

1. Name some of the things Jesus did as He was growing up.

_____

_____

_____

_____

2. **Name some of the things Jesus did not do.**

_____

_____

_____

3. **Give one word that describes Jesus.**

_____

4. **Who was Jesus?** _____

5. **Who sent Jesus to earth?** _____

_____

6. **What was God's purpose in sending Jesus?**
   a. _____
   b. _____

7. **What was the man's name who talked about sin?**

_____

8. **What did John say to the people about repenting (being sorry for their sins)?** _____

_____

9. **Did John say that some people were already good enough and did not need to repent?** _____

_____

10. **What could the people do to show to others that they were sorry for the wrong things they had done and that they wanted to change their ways?**

_____

11. Why did Jesus ask John to baptize Him?

a. _____

b. _____

12. What does being baptized mean?

a. _____

b. _____

c. _____

13. How did God show the people that He had sent Jesus to do something very important on earth?

_____

14. What was the dove a sign of? _____

_____

15. What did the voice of God say from heaven?

_____

_____

 BIBLE FOUNDATIONS   LESSON 4

BIBLE STORY

After Jesus was baptized, He left the crowd of people there and went to be alone with God. He climbed the lonely hills of the desert. Jesus knew that before He would be ready to do God's work and reveal His love to all people, He must go through one final time of preparation.

There in that wilderness, Jesus thought only of God and what God had sent Him to do. He did not eat or drink for forty days and forty nights.

At the end of those long days with no food, Jesus felt hungry. Satan (the devil) had been waiting for this time to try to get Jesus to take another course of action and not follow God's plan. He thought he could trick Him or tempt Him to do what was wrong to do.

"If you are the Son of God," the devil said, "Why don't you command that these stones become bread?"

Jesus knew that with God all things are possible, but He knew by listening to God that God had given Him power only to help others, not to satisfy His own hunger. So Jesus answered Satan and said, "It is written,'Man shall not live by bread alone. He also needs the Words of God for his existence and to satisfy his soul."

Jesus felt very weak but God gave Him the strength He needed to continue to face the devil, Satan took Him into the holy city and sat Him on the highest tower of the Temple. There he urged Jesus again to show that He was the Son of God.

"If you are the Son of God, throw yourself down." Satan reminded Jesus, "It is written that God will take care of You and have His angels be in charge of You so that You will never get hurt."

But Jesus knew again that this would be wrong, because it would not be done to please God, but to test the power of God when God had commanded Him not to do this. It would be for man's glory, not God's. So Jesus said to Satan: "It is written, 'you shall not tempt the Lord your God."

Satan tried in another way to entice Jesus into sinning against God. He took Him to a very high mountain and promised Him that he could rule over all the kingdoms of the world if Jesus would fall down and worship him. Jesus knew this was against God's plan. God would never rule people by forcing His power over them. He would only rule in love.

Jesus said, "Get away, Satan! For it is written, 'you shall worship the Lord your God, and Him only shall you serve'."

The devil had to give up. He knew he was defeated and could not tempt Jesus. As he left Jesus, God's angels came and took care of Him, giving Him food and water and all that He needed.

GUIDED PRAYER THOUGHT

God will help us when we are tempted to do wrong. He gives us strength and power over the enemy.

BIBLE WORDS TO REMEMBER

Man shall not live by bread alone, but by every word of God.
Luke 4:4

WORD MEANINGS

tempted: _____
_____
_____

crowd: _____

reveal: _____

final: _____

preparation: _____

wilderness: _____
_____

Satan: _____
_____

course: _____

command: _____

possible: _____

power: _____

satisfy: _____

written: _____
_____

existence: _____

urged: _____

entice: _____
_____

defeated: _____

QUESTIONS

1. Where did Jesus go after He was baptized? _____
_____

2. Why did He go? _____
_____

3.   How many days and nights did Jesus go without food and water?

_____

4.   What happened after this time? _____

_____

5.   Who came to tempt Him? _____

_____

6.   What did Satan try to get Jesus to do the first time? _____

_____

_____

7.   Even though Jesus was hungry, what did He say?_____

_____

_____

8.   What did Satan try to get Jesus to do the second time?

_____

9.   Did Jesus listen to Satan this time? _____

_____

10.   What was the third temptation? _____

_____

11.   What did Satan promise Jesus if He would do this?

_____

12.   Does God rule with power or love?_____

13.   What was Jesus' response or answer to Satan? _____

_____

14.   What did Jesus say to Satan that finally made him leave Jesus?

_____

15.   Did Satan give up on trying to make Jesus disobey God?

_____

16.   What happened after Satan left Jesus? _____

_____

_____

_____

Challenge:

1.   How many times does Jesus say "It is written?" _____

_____

2.   Where do you see that Satan also used Scripture to trick Jesus?

_____

_____

3.   From this lesson write what the Bible says about "you shall not."

        a. _____

        b. _____

4.   From this lesson give the times that the Bible says "you shall." What are they?

        a. _____

        b. _____

        c. _____

5.   Give another word for 'shall'. _____

6.   What can you do when Satan tells his lies to you?

_____

_____

_____

BIBLE STORY

Jesus was ready to do God's work. He was ready to speak to people about how much God loves them and teach them how God wanted them to live. He knew that many people were hurting inside and there were people who were sick. He wanted to show God's love to them by helping them and healing them from their pain. There were too many people, Jesus thought. I will need others to help me and others who will continue My work after I'm gone.

As Jesus was walking by the Sea of Galilee, He saw two fishermen named Simon (Peter) and Andrew. The brothers were throwing their net into the sea to catch fish. He said to them, "Follow Me, and I will make you fishers of men."

The two men did not hesitate. They left their nets immediately and followed Jesus. They continued walking along the water and Jesus saw two other brothers, James and John, in a boat with their father. They were busy mending their nets because they were also fishermen. Jesus called to them, they left their boat and their father, and followed Jesus.

On the way to Galilee, Jesus and the fishermen met another man named Philip. Jesus said to him, "Follow Me." Philip knew that there was something very special about this man who called to him. He made his decision in a moment to follow Jesus. He ran to get his friend Nathanael. Nathanael had not yet met Jesus and was not convinced. But Philip, without arguing, said "Come and see this man for yourself!"

Jesus saw Nathanael coming and said to him, "I know that you are a true Israelite and you are very honest!" Nathanael was very surprised when Jesus said this and replied, "How did you know me?"

"I saw you under the fig tree before Philip called you", Jesus said. Nathanael was puzzled. He could not understand how Jesus could have seen him because the fig tree was not even close to where Jesus was. He then believed with certainty that Jesus was the promised king of Israel. He said to Jesus, "You are the Son of God!"

Jesus was gentle in His reply to Nathanael but He did reprove him. "Does a small thing like My knowing who you were and that I saw you under the fig tree convince you to believe in Me? You will see much greater things than these."

GUIDED PRAYER

> *Jesus is also calling you He is saying*
> *"follow Me." We are all part of God's plan as*
> *we accept Him and His love for us.*

BIBLE WORDS TO REMEMBER

> *He came to His own, and His own did not receive*
> *Him. but as many as recieved Him, to them He gave*
> *the right to become the children of God,*
> *to those who believe in His name.*
>
> John 1:10

WORD MEANINGS

disciple: _____

_____

not hesitate: _____

_____

immediately: _____

_____

argue: _____

honest: _____

remark: _____

fig tree: _____

certainty: _____

gentle: _____

reply: _____

reprove: _____

QUESTIONS

1. What was Jesus prepared to do? _____

_____

_____

2. What two things were important for Jesus to tell the people?

    a. _____

    b. _____

3. What did Jesus know about the people (including us!)?

    a. _____

    b. _____

4. Where was Jesus walking? _____

_____

5. Who did He see there? _____

6. What were their names? _____
    _____

7. How were they related?_____
    _____

8. What were they doing? _____
    _____

9. What did Jesus say to them? _____
    _____

10. Tell how they responded._____
    _____

11. What did they see then? _____
    _____

12. What were they doing?_____
    _____

13. What was their occupation? _____

14. What did Jesus say to them? _____

15. Did they finish what they were doing and go home first to see
    their mother? _____
    _____

16. Who was the next person Jesus asked to follow Him?
    _____

17. Who came with him, after he met Jesus? _____

18. Why was Nathanael surprised?   _____

_____

19. What did Nathanael say about Jesus? _____

_____

20. What did Jesus say Nathanael would see? _____

_____

Challenge:

1. How would you respond to Jesus if He had come to you as He did
    to the fishermen?_____

    _____

    _____

2. Write a short paragraph putting this story in today's setting.

    _____

    _____

    _____

    _____

    _____

    _____

    _____

    _____

3. How important is it to be ready to hear Jesus calling,
    "Follow Me" and be willing to do what He asks?

    _____

    _____

    _____

BIBLE STORY

Jesus had chosen some of His special followers who believed that He was the Son of God and wanted to be with Him to do God's important work.

Many sick people had come to Jesus for healing. There were blind people, lame people, and people with many different diseases. Crowds of people were following Jesus to hear what He was telling about God. Some people followed Him because they were sad and depressed. Some were looking for the hope that had been promised throughout the Old Testament scriptures. Others were curious about what Jesus had to say and they just wanted to be part of the excitement that surrounded Jesus wherever He was. There were also people who thought that if Jesus was the new king, they would not have to be ruled by the Romans anymore.

Even though many people needed Jesus, He always took time to be alone with God and pray. He knew that communicating with His Father in Heaven was important. This would give His the strength to do what God wanted Him to do. He would go to a quiet place away from His friends and people and all the noise in the towns and   villages and pray.

When His disciples found Him, they urged Him to continue teaching and healing the people. As they walked along the dusty streets of one town, they passed by a man who was collecting taxes. His name was Matthew. Jesus looked at him and knew that Matthew wanted to be different. So Jesus said to him, "follow me". Matthew eagerly left his seat and followed Him. The other disciples knew that everyone hated those who collected taxes. They were often dishonest and kept some of the money for themselves. They wondered why Jesus would ask this man to follow Him.

But Jesus looks on the inside of a person's heart and he knew that Matthew believed in Him and God's message of hope.

Because Jesus had so little time to be here on earth, He knew that He needed to choose some more of His close friends to travel with Him so that they could be His students. He knew that He must teach them and prepare them to continue God's work after He left to go back to heaven.

Jesus prayed that God would show Him which followers to choose. Then He carefully chose twelve men. He used every opportunity to show them what they would need to know and teach them what to tell people about God's kingdom.

GUIDED PRAYER THOUGHTS

Jesus asked for God's guidance even though He was the Son of God! How much more do we need to seek Him, taking time to communicate with Him and listen?

BIBLE WORDS TO REMEMBER

You are the light of the world. Let Your light so shine before men that they may see your good works and glorify your Father in heaven.

Matthew 5:14,16

WORD MEANINGS

lame: _____

diseases: _____

depressed: _____

communicate: _____

eagerly: _____

student: _____

opportunity: _____

QUESTIONS

1. What did the special followers believe? _____

   _____

2. What did they want to do? _____

   _____

3. Who came to Jesus for healing?

   a. _____

   b. _____

   c. _____

4. Who else came to Jesus?

   a. _____

   b. _____

   c. _____

   d. _____

   e. _____

5. **What did Jesus take time to do?**

   a. _____

   b. _____

6. **Why did Jesus do this?** _____

   _____

   _____

7. **Why was this important?**

   a. _____

   b. _____

8. **What kind of a place did Jesus go to?**

   a. _____

   b. _____

   c. _____

9. **What did His disciples do when they found Jesus?** _____

   _____

   _____

10. **Who did they pass by as they were walking?** _____

   _____

   _____

11. **What was His name?** _____

   _____

12. **What did Jesus know about Matthew?** _____

   _____

13. **What did Jesus say to Him?** _____

   _____

14. **What did Matthew do?** _____

_____

15. **What was true of those who collected taxes?** _____

_____

16. **Why were they hated?** _____

_____

17. **What did the other disciples think of Jesus' choice?** _____

_____

_____

18. **What had Jesus been able to do that the disciples could not do?**

_____

19. **What did Jesus see that the disciples could not see?**

_____

_____

_____

20. **Why did Jesus need to choose more close friends?**

_____

21. **What purpose would they have when Jesus left?**

_____

22. **Where would Jesus be?** _____

_____

23. **How did Jesus know which follower's to choose?**

_____

24. How many men did Jesus choose? _____

_____

25. How did Jesus teach them? _____

_____

Challenge:

A. From your Memory Verse:

1. Who are the light of the world? _____

_____

_____

2. What are Christians supposed to do? _____

_____

3. Why? _____

_____

4. What is the purpose of good works? _____

_____

B. Give thought to the following questions:

1. There were different groups of people following Jesus.
      Which one of the groups or categories would you be in?

        a. *People who needed physical healing*

        b. *People who were sad and depressed*

        c. *People who were looking for hope*

        d. *People who were curious*

        e. *People who wanted to be part of the crowd--*
           (liked the excitement)

         f. *People who wanted a new government*

        g. *None of the above*

2. If you circled the letter g, what other category would you consider yourself to be? _____

3. Imagine that you are Matthew. What would be your response to Jesus? Give a reason for your answer. _____

_____

_____

4. What kind of excuses might you give if you decided to say "No" to Jesus? _____

_____

5. Jesus has chosen YOU. He is saying to you, "Follow Me." What will your answer be? _____

_____

6. As you think of opportunity, would you consider that we must have the same urgency that Jesus had in doing what God wants us to do with the short time we have?

_____

_____

_____

BIBLE STORY

In the Old Testament we read again and again (I hope you were able to study the Old Testament first!) about how much God loved His people, the Israelites. He tried in so many ways to show them His love and how much He cared for them.

But time after time, they remembered God and His commandments and then after receiving His many blessings, they forgot and chose to disobey. They turned to other gods and worshiped idols instead of the one true God. God was very sad. The people just could not understand His great love for them.

So God sent Jesus. Jesus came to our world to show us God's love in a way we could understand. Jesus was God's own Son, sent from heaven. God will not give up loving us! The message Jesus came to give is really only one word: LOVE.

Jesus brought this message of God's love first to His own people in Nazareth where he grew up with His family. He read from the scriptures in the synagogue:

> "The spirit of the Lord is upon Me,
> Because He has anointed Me
> To preach good news to the poor;
> He has sent me to heal the brokenhearted
> To proclaim liberty to the captives
> And recovery of sight to the blind,
> To set at liberty those who are oppressed.

The people listened as Jesus said, "I am the One whom God has sent." There was astonishment at the words He spoke. Jesus realized that these people could not understand that He was the Son of God. His message would be rejected among His own people. They would not accept Him as the Son of God.

Jesus knew He would need to take His message to other towns and villages, continuing until He reached the city of Jerusalem. Many people would listen and believe. Those without hope would know that Jesus had come to make their sadness go away. They would know that their lives could change and they would understand how to live to please God.

There were many other people who would listen, but would not believe. They would continue to try to please God in their own way; ways that would not work and were not acceptable to God.

GUIDED PRAYER THOUGHTS

Help us to understand
that God will keep on loving us but because of
His great love, we will love and
follow His commandments and obey Him.
We need to ask His forgiveness when we hurt others.
We need to ask God to help us remember what is
most important.

BIBLE WORDS TO REMEMBER

Do not lay up for yourselves treasures on earth; but lay
up for yourselves treasures in heaven. For where your
treasure is, there your heart will be also. But seek first the
kingdom of God and His righteousness, and all these
things shall be added to you. Do not worry about
tomorrow, for tomorrow will worry about its own things.
Matthew 6: 19-20
33, 34

No one can serve two masters; for either he will hate the
one and love the other, or else he will be loyal to the one
and despise the other. You cannot serve God and mammon.
Matthew 6: 24

WORD MEANINGS

brokenhearted: _____

proclaim: _____

liberty: _____

captives: _____

recovery: _____

oppressed: _____

rejected: _____

astonishment: _____

acceptable: _____

loyal: _____

despise: _____

mammon: _____

synagogue: _____

QUESTIONS

1. **What do we learn about God in the Old Testament?**

   _____

   _____

   _____

2. **What do we learn about people in the Old Testament?**

   a. _____

   b. _____

   c. _____

3. **Were the people in the Old Testament a lot different than people in the New Testament and the people today?** _____

   _____

   _____

4. How does God feel when people forget? _____

5. What does God want people to understand? _____

     _____

     _____

6. What did God do to help people understand His love?

     _____

7. Will God give up trying to show how much He loves us?

     _____

     _____

     _____

8. Where did Jesus give His message first? _____

     _____

9. Where did He speak? _____

     _____

10. What words did He speak? _____

     _____

11. Did the people in Nazareth believe that Jesus was the one talked about in the scripture whom God had sent?

     _____

12. What did the people do?   _____

     _____

13. What did Jesus know He would need to do? _____

     _____

14. What would happen then? _____

_____

Challenge:

1. Write down all of the things God did in this lesson.

      a. _____

      b. _____

      c. _____

      d. _____

      e. _____

      f. _____

2. Write down all of the things Jesus did in this lesson.

      a. _____

      b. _____

      c. _____

      d. _____

      e. _____

3. Give the differences in the two types of people who listened to Jesus:

    a. Those who believed:

_____

_____

_____

    b. Those who did not:

_____

_____

_____

4. How will you respond personally to Jesus and His message of God's love? _____

   _____

   _____

5. Who are you trying to serve? The Bible words you have learned tell us that No one can serve two_____, for either he will _____the one and _____the other, or else he will be _____ to the one and_____the other. You cannot serve _____ and _____ .

6. What words in the above verse are opposites?

   a. _____   _____

   b. _____   _____

   c. _____   _____

7. Try to identify what mammon is in your life and decide how you will ask God to help you know what to do about it.

   _____

   _____

   _____

8. What did you learn in Matthew 6:34 about being concerned?

   _____

   _____

BIBLE STORY

God loves all people, everywhere. Jesus came to bring God's message of love to not only the Israelites, God's chosen people but to the whole world. We read in the Bible that God so loved the world, that He gave His only Son, so that whoever believes in Him will live forever!

Jesus gave the message of hope and love to everyone, even a woman from Samaria. To help understand why this story is unusual there are some facts you should know. The Samaritans were not part of the nation of Israel and there were bad feelings between the Israelites and the Samaritans. They really hated each other. They were never allowed to be friends, and did not speak to each other. They would even travel out of their way to avoid meeting each other. Now the rest of the story......

Jesus decided to travel right through Samaria and had stopped by a well to rest. He was very hungry and thirsty. His disciples had gone into a nearby village to buy food. As He was waiting for their return, a Samaritan woman came to the well with her jar to get water. Jesus asked her for a drink.

The woman was very surprised that Jesus, an Israelite (Jew) would speak with her. Jesus said, "If you knew the gift of God and who it is that is saying to you, 'give Me a drink', you would have asked Him, and He would have given you living water." When she noticed that He had no jar in which to get water, she asked Him, "Where do you get the living water?"

Jesus said to her, "Everyone who drinks of this water will be thirsty again, but whoever drinks of the water that I shall give him, will never be thirsty again; the water I give will be like a well of water springing up into everlasting life."

The woman said, "Sir, give me this water, so that I will never be thirsty again." Jesus told her many things that she had done in her life that a stranger could not know and the woman knew He must have power from God. She spoke again, "I know that One is coming who will show us all things and He will be called "The Christ."

Then Jesus said, "I am the ONE."

The woman ran into the town to tell others about Jesus and said "I have found the Christ!" Many of those people went to find Jesus and listened to Him and believed that He was the Son of God, The Christ.

GUIDED PRAYER THOUGHTS

We thank you God, that you have loved the world--even loved us all enough to send your very Own Son to show us that love. Help us show Your love to others around us everywhere--not to just the people we like. Show us how to love and not judge others.
In Jesus' Name, Amen

BIBLE WORDS TO REMEMBER

Important things Jesus taught:
Judge not, that you be not judged. For with what judgment you judge you will be judged.
Matthew 7:1-2

Ask, and it will be given to you; seek, and you will find; knock, and it will be opened to you.
Matthew 7:7

WORD MEANINGS

Israelites: _____

forever: _____

hope: _____

understand: _____

unusual: _____

Samaritans: _____
_____

avoid: _____

everlasting: _____

living water: _____
_____

springing: _____

stranger: _____

The Christ: _____

QUESTIONS

1. Whom does God love? _____

2. What did God do to show His love? _____

3. To whom did Jesus give God's message of hope and love?

   _____
   _____

4. Tell five facts about the Samaritans and Jews that make this story unusual.

   a. _____
   b. _____
   c. _____
   d. _____
   e. _____

5. Where did Jesus travel? _____

6. Where was Jesus resting? _____

7. Where were the disciples? _____

8. Who else came to the well? _____

9. What was she carrying? _____

10. For what purpose was the jar?_____

11. What did Jesus ask the woman? _____

12. How did the woman respond when Jesus spoke to her?

_____

13. Why was it unusual for Jesus to talk to a Samaritan?

_____

14. What did Jesus say about water? _____

_____

15. Was the woman interested in the water Jesus had? _____

_____

16. What was different about the water she could drink and the water Jesus could give? _____

17. Who did Jesus say that He was?_____

18. Did the woman believe that Jesus was the Christ? _____

19. What did the woman do when she realized she had been talking to Jesus, the Christ? _____

20.   What was the response of the people she told?_____

BIBLE STORY

Jesus taught His disciples and the people who gathered to hear Him with simple words. He did not make the Good News complicated or difficult to understand. What He taught on the mountainside became the basic guide for all those who believed then and those who now believe in Jesus.

On this special day, Jesus and His disciples had climbed to the top of a hillside. Others had followed and listened as Jesus told them some very important words. He began with what are now called the Beatitudes which means 'The way to happiness'. This is the sermon Jesus gave.

> Blessed are the poor in spirit
>   For theirs is the kingdom of heaven.
> Blessed are those who mourn
>   For they shall be comforted.
> Blessed are the meek
>   For they shall inherit the earth.
> Blessed are those who hunger and thirst
>   after righteousness
>   For they shall be filled.
> Blessed are the merciful
>   For they shall obtain mercy.
> Blessed are the pure in heart,
>   For they shall see God.
> Blessed are the peacemakers,
>   For they shall be called sons of God.
> Blessed are those who are persecuted for
>   righteousness sake,
> For theirs is the kingdom of heaven.

Many people want to be happy. They expect someone to give them happiness. The question is often asked, "How can I be happy?" Jesus told us the answer in the Beatitudes. You cannot be made happy by what you get, but by what you are---attitude has a lot to do with what you are. Believing in Jesus as your savior is the first and most important thing we do because it is only through Him that we can know who we really are.

The key to happiness is what is in your heart! It is not having money or the things money will buy. It is thinking first of God and how He wants you to treat others. Jesus said that even if you are sad at times, your heart can be full of joy because you are loving God and doing the right thing.

Jesus also said, "It's not just doing the right thing, but thinking what is right. He said, "You must love everyone, even your enemies!

GUIDED PRAYER THOUGHT

Love your enemies, bless those who curse you, do good to those who hate you, and pray for those who spitefully use you and persecute you.

Matthew 5:44

You shall love the Lord your God with all your heart, with all your soul, and with all your mind. You shall love your neighbor as yourself.

Matthew 22:37

BIBLE WORDS TO REMEMBER

Dear Heavenly Father,
Forgive us for thinking only of ourselves instead of others.
Help us to love others as You love them and teach
us to do right. Amen

WORD MEANINGS

Beatitude: _____

guide: _____

sermon: _____

blessed: _____

mourn: _____

comforted: _____

meek: _____

inherit: _____

merciful: _____

mercy: _____

peacemaker: _____

persecuted: _____

righteous: _____

attitude: _____

curse: _____

spitefully: _____

QUESTIONS

1. What kind of words did Jesus use to teach? _____

2. Why did Jesus teach people this way? _____

_____

_____

3. What did Jesus teach on the mountainside? _____

4. Who was this teaching meant for?

    a. _____

    b. _____

5. What does the word Beatitude mean? _____

_____

6. Make a list of those who will be happy (blessed).

    a. _____

    b. _____

    c. _____

    d. _____

    e. _____

    f. _____

    g. _____

    h. _____

7. Make a corresponding list (beside each of the above) and tell what these will receive.

    a. _____

    b. _____

    c. _____

    d. _____

    e. _____

    f. _____

    g. _____

    h. _____

8. Which words are repeated? _____

9. For whom are these words said?

    a. _____

    b. _____

10. How many times is the word 'blessed' used? _____

11. Can 'things' or money make us happy? _____

12. Can other people make you happy? _____

13. What did Jesus say would make you happy?

      a. _____

      b. _____

14. What will happen when we think first of God? _____

      _____

15. What will happen when we think of others before we think of ourselves? _____

16. Did Jesus say that we will be good if we 'do' the right thing?

      _____

17. Who did Jesus say we must love? _____

18. What should we do for those who treat us in the wrong way?

      _____

      19. How should we love God?

           a. _____

           b. _____

           c. _____

20. How should we love our neighbor? _____

      _____

**BIBLE
STORY**

As Jesus continued His teaching on the mountain, He said many things that made people stop and think about what it means to be a follower of Jesus. He said, "Love your enemies." How can you love someone who hates you and does wrong things to you?

When you love someone, you want only what is best for them. You are willing to help them get the best things. Now, Jesus is telling us that instead of wanting the worst things to happen to those who do wrong, you can want the best things to happen to them. This sounds very difficult to do and that is why Jesus says He will always be with us, helping us to do and think kind thoughts if we ask Him.

Jesus showed us His example when people hurt Him and we will learn how much He suffered because He loved us in another lesson. But instead of hating the people who hurt and killed Him, He asked God to forgive them.

Jesus also gave the most important rule for how to treat others. It is called The Golden Rule which says,
"Whatever you want someone to do
to you, do the same to them."

Jesus said that if you believe and do what God commands, you are like a light in the world. He said to "let your light shine for everyone so that they will see your goodness and will glorify your Father in heaven."

Some people didn't understand what Jesus meant about what they should do to be in God's kingdom. Jesus said it wasn't being rich. He said the poor would be welcome in God's kingdom. It wasn't the people who went to church and thought they were religious. The most important thing in being a part of God's kingdom is to know you have sinned against God and telling Him that you know you have done wrong (everyone has!). You must ask Him into your life to be your king (Savior). Then you will want to follow God's ways so that you will be able to enter God's heavenly kingdom to live forever.

One day, while Jesus was teaching, mothers brought their little children to Him. They wanted their children to see Jesus and have Jesus bless them. The disciples told the mothers and children to go away because Jesus was too busy.

Jesus heard the disciples tell them to go and He said, "Do not tell them to leave. Let the children come to Me because in God's kingdom there are many children. Everyone who comes to God's kingdom must trust God just as a little child."

GUIDED PRAYER THOUGHTS

Dear God, sometimes it is very hard to love someone who is mean and says unkind things. Help us to remember that You want us to treat others as we want to be treated. We know that You will help us if we ask. We love you.
In Jesus' Name, Amen

BIBLE WORDS TO REMEMBER

And just as you want others to do to you, you also do to them likewise.

Luke 6:31

Jesus said, Let the little children come to Me, and do not forbid them; for of such is the kingdom of heaven.

Matthew 19:14

WORD MEANINGS

difficult: _____

example: _____

suffered: _____

treat: _____

forgive: _____

welcome: _____

likewise: _____

forbid: _____

gospels: _____

Phrase Meaning

Kingdom of God: Many of our lessons in the Gospels speak of the kingdom of God. This term means all people who believe in Jesus and belong to Him will be in God's kingdom over which He will rule forever.

QUESTIONS

1. Where was Jesus teaching? _____

2. What did people have to consider when they listened to what He was saying? _____

3. Is it always easy to be a follower of Jesus? _____

   _____

4. Think of the people you love (mom, dad, grandparents) What do you want for them? _____

   _____

   _____

5. What does Jesus say that we should want for everyone not just those we love? _____

_____

_____

6. Can we act and think kindly toward those who are not nice to us all by ourselves? _____

_____

_____

7. How did Jesus show us how to do this?_____

_____

8. What did He ask God to do? _____

9. What important rule did Jesus give us? _____

10. How are we supposed to treat other people?_____

_____

11. If we follow God's commands, what did Jesus say we were like?

_____

12. What did Jesus say we should do?_____

13. Tell the two reasons we should do this.

      a. _____

      b. _____

14. What things did Jesus say were not important to get into God's kingdom?

      a. _____

      b. _____

15. What things are most important to be a part of God's kingdom?

a. _____

b. _____

c. _____

d. _____

16. What will happen when we do the most important things?

_____

17. What did the mothers in this story do? _____

18. What did the disciples say to the mothers? _____

_____

19. What did Jesus say that showed He did not like what the disciples had said? _____

20. What did Jesus say about children and the kingdom?

a. _____

b. _____

 # BIBLE FOUNDATIONS LESSON 11

BIBLE STORY

The disciples often saw Jesus go to a quiet place for prayer. They knew that He received strength and peace and a renewed spirit from these times alone with God. He also was assured of His purpose.

They asked Jesus to teach them how to pray. He said that they should remember the reason for praying; that prayer is not something you do so that you can be seen in front of a lot of other people. It is talking to God with reverence and honor. It is letting Him know what is in your heart, asking forgiveness and asking Him to show you His will.

Jesus gave an example in His prayer that we may follow in our prayers to God:

> Our Father in Heaven
> Hallowed be Your Name.
> Your kingdom come.
> Your will be done
> On earth as it is in heaven.
> Give us this day our daily bread.
> And forgive us our debts,
> As we forgive our debtors.
> And do not lead us into temptation,
> But deliver us from the evil one.
> For Yours is the kingdom and
> The power and the glory
> > Forever.
> > > Amen.

Remember that prayer is much more than asking God for things we want. Jesus' prayer shows us five important parts to include when we pray:
1) Praise
2) Thanking

3) Confession
4) Asking for God's Help
5) Praying for others

Jesus continued teaching the people on the mountain with little word pictures to help them know and understand how they should live. He told a story of two builders, one wise and one foolish.

He said that everyone who heard His words and would do them is like the wise man who built his house on a rock. He carefully laid a good, solid foundation. When the rain, wind and floods came, the house stood firm.

Then He told the second part of the story:
Everyone who hears My words and does not do them is like a foolish man who built his house on the sand. When the rain, wind and floods came, this man's house was destroyed.

Jesus knew that some people would listen to Him and go away and forget everything He told them; and that some people who remembered what He said would ignore His words. He wanted the people to understand how important it was to know that God's commandments were like a firm and solid foundation on which to build their life and that when they listened and followed what He was teaching them, they would have peace and contentment.

GUIDED PRAYER THOUGHTS

> *The key to remember in prayer is that when we have a personal relationship with God through Jesus Christ, our prayers can be expressed from the heart. Since He knows our thoughts, we can tell Him anything and He will understand.*

BIBLE WORDS TO REMEMBER

> *Memorize the Lord's Prayer*
> Matthew 6:9-13

WORD MEANINGS

renewed: _____

assured: _____

purpose: _____

reverence: _____

Hallowed: _____

debts: _____

debtors: _____

evil one: _____

confession: _____

foolish: _____

wise: _____

foundation: _____

firm: _____

QUESTIONS

1. Where did Jesus usually go to pray? _____

   _____

2. What did Jesus receive from God during these times?

   a. _____

   b. _____

   c. _____

   d. _____

3. What did the disciples ask Jesus to teach them? _____

4. What two things did Jesus emphasize before He taught them the words to say?

   a. _____

   b. _____

5. How should we talk to God?

   a. _____

   b. _____

6. What other things do we know about prayer from the lesson?

   a. _____

   b. _____

   c. _____

7. Why did Jesus pray this prayer (often called The Lord's Prayer)?

   _____

8. How many requests at the beginning are about God? _____

9. **What are they?**

        a. _____

        b. _____

        c. _____

10. **How many requests are for ourselves?** _____

11. **What are they?**

        a. _____

        b. _____

        c. _____

        d. _____

12. **Is the purpose of prayer to get the things we want?** _____

    _____

13. **What are the five important parts in Jesus' prayer?**

        a. _____

        b. _____

        c. _____

        d. _____

        e. _____

14. **Write or say your own prayer using these five things.**

    _____

    _____

    _____

    _____

    _____

15. **After Jesus talked about prayer what did He do?** _____

    _____

16. How did He teach to help them understand how they should live?

   _____

17. What story using this way of teaching did He tell?

   _____

18. Where did the wise man build his house? _____

19. Where did the foolish man build his house? _____

20. What happened to each house when the wind and floods came?

   a. _____
   b. _____

22. What did Jesus say about people who heard His words?

   a. _____
   b. _____
   c. _____

23. Which people can you compare with the wise man? _____

   _____

24. Which people are compared with the foolish man?

   a. _____
   b. _____

25. Which kind of listener are you or should you want to be?

   _____

   _____

   _____

BIBLE STORY

In the Bible there are many stories or parables that Jesus told. (There are about forty in the New Testament.) All of these stories were to teach the people and help them understand the truths in the lessons Jesus gave. He was a wonderful teacher and the people loved to listen and discover what the stories meant.

One day a man asked Jesus a question. This man thought that he could trick Jesus into saying something that would be foolish. He asked, "What shall I do to have everlasting life?"

Jesus responded with a question for him. "What is written in the scripture? You have read the Holy Book, tell me what it says."

The man had been to school and thought He had learned many things. He was arrogant, thinking he knew all the answers to hard questions. So he said to Jesus, "It says, love God with all your heart and with all your soul and with all your strength; and you shall love your neighbor as yourself." After he finished, he was disappointed that Jesus did not argue. Then he said, "And who is my neighbor?"

Jesus answered this question with a parable, but to understand this story you must know two things. The first is that the road in the story was a dangerous one. Robbers were often there because there were places along the road where they could hide and then jump out to rob their victims. The second thing you must know is that the Jews and Samaritans hated each other as we have heard in the lesson about the Samaritan woman at the well where Jesus was.

The story is based on the fact that both hated each other, and never did anything kind or even would speak to each other.

This is what Jesus told:
A man was walking along the road from Jerusalem to Jericho. Robbers attacked him and beat him until he was almost dead. A priest came along on his way to worship at the temple. He saw the hurt man but walked on the other side of the road and pretended not to see him.

Another religious man came along who was also going to worship God. He came close to the wounded man and thought, 'poor fellow—he looks pretty beat up, it's too bad I don't have time to help him but I'll be late if I stop. He went on his way.

The next person who came along was a Samaritan. He could have said, 'I would have helped him, but he's a Jew!' But he did not say that. Instead, he stopped and took care of his wounds. Then he carried him on his own donkey and took him to an inn and paid for his room and took care of him.

Then Jesus asked those who were listening: "Who was the neighbor of the man who was robbed?"

The man who had asked Jesus the question did not like the answer he would have to give. "It was the one who helped; it was the Samaritan."

Jesus said, "Then you must do the same."

GUIDED PRAYER THOUGHT

Dear God, Help us to listen and understand Your words to us. We want to learn to love others as You want us to. Forgive us for being selfish and thinking only of ourselves.

BIBLE WORDS TO REMEMBER

You shall love the Lord your God with all your heart, with all your soul, with all your mind, and your neighbor as yourself.

Luke 10:27

WORD MEANINGS

parables: _____

arrogant: _____

argue: _____

victims: _____

wounded: _____

inn: _____

QUESTIONS

1. What is a parable? _____

2. How many parables are in the New Testament?_____

3. What does a parable help us do? _____

4. How did the people feel about listening to Jesus?_____

_____

_____

5. What did they like to do as they listened? _____

_____

_____

6. What was the question that caused Jesus to tell a story in this
    lesson? _____

_____

7. Why did the man ask this question? _____

_____

8. How did Jesus respond? _____

9. What was the question Jesus asked him? _____

_____

10. Did this man know what the scriptures said? _____

_____

11. After the man told Jesus what the scripture said, what else did he
    ask?_____

12. What two things did we need to know to understand the story
    Jesus told in answer to the man's question?

    a. _____

    b. _____

13. In what other lesson did we hear the word 'Samaritan'?

_____

14. Give the first event in the story. _____

_____

15. What did the first man (a priest) do when he saw what had happened?

_____

16. Why didn't the second man stop to help? _____

17. What three things did the third person do?

      a. _____

      b. _____

      c. _____

18. What question did Jesus ask?_____

19. Why do you think the man was not happy with the answer he had to give? _____

_____

20. Which of the three who passed by would God want you be?

_____

21. Can you think of a time that you helped someone when it would have been easier not to? _____

_____

BIBLE STORY

Matthew 18:23

Jesus always told stories (parables) that had a purpose. The meaning is very important because Jesus knows how unhappy people are when they do not believe that God has a wonderful plan for everyone. If they do not follow Him, they will never know true happiness or be able to live forever with Him in heaven. We need to choose to follow Jesus. He will never force us or make us love Him.

Jesus wants people's lives to change so they will not only know who God is, but they will have faith that by trusting Him as their Savior, they can continue to live to please God.

Peter, one of Jesus' first disciples, asked Jesus about forgiveness. He said to Jesus, "If someone keeps doing wrong against me, how many times do I have to forgive him? Should I forgive him seven times?"

Jesus said, "not seven times, but up to seventy times seven." Then Jesus told this story about forgiveness. He said, "the kingdom of God is like a certain king who wanted to settle his accounts with his servants. One of the servants owed him ten thousand talents (that's a lot of money!). But because he was not able to pay, his master commanded that he be sold, with his wife and children and all that he had so that the payment could be made. The servant then fell down on his knees before him and begged, "Master, have patience with me, and I will pay you all I owe!"

The master felt very sorry for the servant. He released him and forgave him all the money he owed, saying, "you will not have to pay me, because I forgive you."

But then that same servant went out and found another fellow servant who owed him a hundred denari. The first servant laid hands on him and took him by the throat, saying, "pay me what you owe!" His fellow servant fell down at his feet and begged him saying, "Have patience with me, and I will pay you everything I owe you."

And he would not, but went and threw him into prison until he should pay the debt. When the other servants saw what had been done, they were very sad, and came and told their master all that had happened.

Then the master called to the one who did this and said to him, "You wicked servant! I forgave you all your debt because you begged me. would you not also have had compassion on your fellow servant, just as I had pity on you?" The master was angry, and delivered him to the jail until he should pay all that was due to him."

Jesus ended this story by saying that if we do not forgive others, God will not forgive us.

GUIDED PRAYER THOUGHT

Dear God, We know that we will never be happy unless we follow your plan. Help us to understand how much You love us and learn to forgive others the way you forgive us. In Jesus Name, Amen

BIBLE WORDS TO REMEMBER

Therefore be merciful, just as your father also is merciful. Judge not, and you shall not be judged. Condemn not, and you shall not be condemned. Forgive, and you will be forgiven.

Luke 6:36-37

WORD MEANINGS

purpose: _____

force: _____

change: _____

faith: _____

trust: _____

Savior: _____

continue: _____

forgive: _____

_____

settle: _____

accounts: _____

owed: _____

_____

talent(money): _____

denari(money): _____

_____

_____

released: _____

wicked: _____

compassion: _____

pity: _____

QUESTIONS

1. What was unique about the stories Jesus told? _____

_____

2. What awareness did Jesus have about people? _____

_____

_____

3. What three things will we know if we follow God?

   a. _____

   b. _____

   c. _____

4. How can we come to God? _____

5. What will God never do? _____

6. What does Jesus want for us?

   a. _____

   b. _____

7. What will happen when we do this? _____

_____

_____

8. What did Peter want to know about? _____

9. What question did he ask? _____

_____

10. What did Peter think would be a reasonable (or generous) number? _____

11. What did Jesus say? _____

12. What characters were in the story Jesus told?

    a. _____

    b. _____

    c. _____

    d. _____

13. What happened when the servant could not pay the money he owed? _____

_____

14. What did this servant do? _____

15. What did he beg? _____

_____

16. Did the king then give him the punishment? _____

_____

17. What did the servant have to pay? _____

_____

18. When the servant left his master, what did he do?

_____

19. Compare the amount of money this man owed with the first servant's debt. _____

20. **What circumstances were similar?**

       a. _____

       b. _____

21. **What response was different than the first?**

       a. _____

       b. _____

22. **How did the master find out what happened?** _____

_____

23. **How did they feel about what happened?** _____

24. **What did the master do to the wicked servant?**

_____

25. **What did he remind the servant of?**

       a. _____

       b. _____

       c. _____

       d. _____

26. **What did the master do with this servant?** _____

_____

27. **What is to be learned from this story?** _____

_____

_____

Jesus had difficulty making the people understand what He meant by the Kingdom of God. When He talked about the kingdom of God, they were thinking about a great empire like the Romans had, with a king and a court and an army that was very powerful.

But Jesus was talking about the rule of God in people's lives with God being the king of their hearts and all their thoughts. He meant for people to make God the very most important in all they did because they loved Him and wanted to serve Him.

As we have learned already, Jesus tried many different ways to help them understand. Here is another kingdom story that Jesus told. See if you can tell what the meaning is.

> The kingdom of heaven is like a man
> traveling to a far country. He called
> to his servants and delivered his goods
> to them. To one he gave five talents,
> to another two and to another, one.
> Each was given according to his own
> ability. Then he left to go on his
> journey.

The one who had received five went and traded with them and made another five talents. The man who had received two also gained two more. But the man who had received one went and dug in the ground, and hid his lord's money.

When the master returned, he called his servants to settle the accounts with them. The one who had received five talents said to him, 'Lord, you gave me five talents; look, I have gained five more talents.' His lord said to him, 'Well done, good and faithful servant; you were faithful over a few things, I will make you ruler over many things. Enter into the joy of your lord.'

The one who had received two talents came and said, Lord, you gave me two talents; look, I have gained two more talents besides them.' His lord said to him, 'Well done, good and faithful servant; you have been faithful over a few things, I will make you ruler over many things. Enter into the joy of your lord.'

Then the one who had received one talent came and said, 'Lord, I knew you were a hard man and I was afraid, and went and hid your talent in the ground. Look, there you have what is yours.'

But the master was not happy with the third servant. He said, 'You wicked and lazy servant, you should have at least put my money in the bank to earn interest! So the talent was taken from him and given to the one who had ten talents.

Jesus ended this story by saying that we should use what we have been given wisely. Those who waste what they have will end up with nothing at all. We should carefully use what God gave for good things and not misuse our minds and bodies on things that are not important in God's kingdom. The Bible says we have each been given more than money. There are many good gifts that God has given us. The greatest gift is the gift of Love.

Jesus was telling the people that each one should make the best use of what they have been given. It is not only money, but the many good gifts that God has given. We should carefully use what God gave for good things and not misuse our minds and bodies on things that are not important in God's kingdom.

GUIDED PRAYER THOUGHT

Dear God, we know that You have given each of us special gifts that we should use for Your Glory. Help us to know and understand how important it is to not waste what You have given.... and help us most of all, to be a channel for the most important gift of all, Your LOVE!

BIBLE WORDS TO REMEMBER

For everyone to whom much is given, from him much will be required; and to whom much has been committed, of him they will ask the more.

Luke 12:48

WORD MEANINGS

kingdom of God;
kingdom of heaven: _____

_____

empire: _____

court: _____

talents; money: _____

talents; gifts: _____

according: _____

ability: _____

traded: _____

faithful: _____

hard: _____

earn interest: _____

misuse: _____

channel: _____

committed: _____

least: _____

diversities: _____

ministries: _____

QUESTIONS

1. What did some people want the kingdom of God to mean?

   _____

2. What did Jesus mean when He talked about the Kingdom of God or the kingdom of heaven? _____

   _____

   _____

3. Can you remember some of the other stories in which Jesus told to help us understand what God's kingdom was like?

   a. _____

   b. _____

   c. _____

4. What did you learn from each of those stories?

   a. _____

   b. _____

   c. _____

5. What are the stories Jesus told called? _____

6. What is different about the stories Jesus told and stories that are made up to entertain? _____

   _____

7. Could people always understand what Jesus was trying to teach them? _____

8. In the story Jesus told in today's lesson, what did the master do before he left on a trip? _____

9. What did he give the first servant? _____

10. What was given to the second servant? _____

11. How much money was given to the third? _____

12. Why were they given different amounts? _____

    _____

13. How many servants were wise with what they had been given?

    _____

14. Which ones were wise and why?

    a. _____

    b. _____

15. What was the master's response to these servants?

    _____

16. What did he say about their faithfulness? _____

    _____

17. What would be their reward? _____

    _____

18. What did the other servant do with what he had been given?

    _____

19. What reason did he give for what he did? _____

20. What did the master say to him? _____

21. What did he say was the least he could have done?

_____

22. What did the master do? _____

23. What lesson was Jesus teaching? _____

_____

24. What other gifts has God given besides money? _____

_____

25. What does the Bible say is the most important gift? _____

Challenge:

1. Think of the gifts (talents and abilities) God has given you and list at least several; you have many! _____

_____

_____

_____

_____

2. Tell how you can use each of these gifts for God. _____

_____

_____

_____

3. Explain or write in your own words what the Bible words to remember mean to you. Luke 12:48: _____

_____

_____

_____

BIBLE STORY

There were many kinds of people that followed Jesus and listened to Him teach and tell parables, stories with a meaning. Some were farmers, some were fishermen; there were business people, children, shepherds, politicians, religious people, tax collectors and even Roman soldiers. Some of the religious people could not understand why Jesus would talk and even eat dinner with those they thought were terrible 'sinners'. They said, "Why does He associate with the wrong kind of people?" But the Bible tells us that everyone has sinned. There is not one that has not done wrong things.

Jesus was concerned with both the good and bad. He said that He had come to help those who were sick, not those who were already healthy. Then Jesus told a story to illustrate His point that God loves everyone. This story is told about a lost sheep.

To help you understand the story, there are some facts about shepherds that you need to know:

Shepherds lived a difficult and lonely life. They had to stay up on the hillside with the sheep even if it rained or the wind was blowing hard. Some shepherds owned their own sheep; others took care of sheep for rich owners. The shepherd had to lead the flock of sheep to meadows where the waters flowed slowly to make the grass sweet and fresh. He had to keep a special watch over the little lambs and carefully take care of the mother sheep who was soon to give birth to their lambs.

Many people in that day owned small flocks of sheep. The owner knew all of his sheep by name because some of the sheep had lived many years and the shepherd knew each one.

Jesus began His parable: "There was a shepherd who owned one hundred sheep. One night he brought them home to be put safely in their fold. But as he counted, he discovered that one was missing. He thought to himself, 'Can that be right—only ninety-nine sheep?' Maybe he had missed one coming into the fold. He decided to count again. This was very difficult because, of course, the sheep would not be still; they were bumping and jumping. The shepherd counted once again. Only ninety-nine! He was very sad. He said, 'I will go back and look for the one who is lost.

He looked everywhere for the sheep. His hands and legs were scratched from the thorns in the bushes. His feet were scraped and hurting from the rough rocks. The wind started to blow hard. Finally, when he had almost given up hope, he thought he heard a low bleating. Could it be his sheep? He listened carefully and went toward the sound.

He called to his sheep and the sheep knew the sound of his shepherd's voice. He continued to bleat until the shepherd climbed to the spot where the sheep was caught in the thorns of a bush.

It took a long time to free the sheep from where he was. The sheep was bleeding and lame, but the shepherd gently held him in his arms and carried him home.

The family came running when they saw the shepherd and his sheep returning. They were so happy! The sheep was safe!" They called their neighbors to come and celebrate with them.

Jesus looked at His listeners. "I am telling you," He said, "that there is joy just like that in heaven when one per-son comes to God—-that is how much He loves each one." Jesus is like our shepherd. He looks for us and calling those who are lost, wanting them to be home with Him and safe forever—He cares that much.

GUIDED PRAYER THOUGHT

Dear Father in Heaven, we want to thank You for caring about us so much! Thank You for Your love and for sending Jesus to show us what Your love is. Help us to listen for our Good Shepherd and always follow Him. In Jesus Name, Amen.

BIBLE WORDS TO REMEMBER

For the Son of Man has come to save that which was lost. Even so it is not the will of your Father who is in heaven that one of these little ones should perish.

Matthew 18:11;14

WORD MEANINGS

politicians: _____

religious: _____

_____

_____

hypocrite: _____

_____

associate: _____

concerned: _____

illustrate: _____

_____

fold: _____

astray: _____

assuredly: _____

perish: _____

QUESTIONS

1. **Name the kinds of people who were listening as Jesus told this story.**

    a. _____

    b. _____

    c. _____

    d. _____

    e. _____

    f. _____

    g. _____

    h. _____

    i. _____

    j. _____

2. **Tell how the story would have meaning for each category of people, not just the shepherds.**

    a. _____

    b. _____

    c. _____

    e. _____

    f. _____

    g. _____

    h. _____

    i. _____

    j. _____

3. **Which of these people did Jesus associate with?**_____

4. **Why was Jesus criticized?** _____

5. **Who was considered by some to be the 'bad people'?** _____

    _____

    _____

6. **What did Jesus want the people to understand by telling the story of the Lost Sheep?** _____

7. **Why did the shepherd care so much about the one lost sheep when he had ninety-nine left?** _____

   _____

8. **How is this like God?** _____

9. **How well did the shepherd know his sheep?** _____

   _____

10. **What condition was the sheep in when the shepherd found it?**

    _____

11. **Was the shepherd angry that the sheep had strayed?** _____

    _____

    _____

12. **What happened when the shepherd returned home with the lost sheep?** _____

13. **What did Jesus say that the angels in heaven do when a sinner comes to God?** _____

14. **Who is our Good Shepherd?** _____

15. **What should we always do?** _____

    _____

16. **Why do you think this story is important?** _____

    _____

BIBLE STORY

There was a man who had not been able to walk for many years. Every day he lay in the darkness of his room on his mat. Sometimes his friends would come and carry his mat outside so that he could see the bright sunshine and the blue sky. They wanted to cheer him up and make him feel better.

One day, the town seemed strangely quiet. Everyone had left to go somewhere but where, the man wondered, did they go? He felt even more depressed and lonely. Sadness rushed over him until he heard voices outside and his four good friends came rushing into his house.

"Jesus is in our town!" they shouted. "We want to take you to see Him." Before the man could say, "I can't go", his friends had picked up each corner of his mat and carried him carefully out through the door.

When they reached the house where Jesus was, the crowds were pushing and jumping up, trying to get a glimpse of Jesus from the door. How would the friends ever get close enough to get their sick friend to Jesus?

But the four friends were determined and would not give up. They thought of a plan.

"Let's go up on the roof—we can make a hole in the roof and let him down in front of Jesus."

Because the roof was made of mud and straw, their work was done quickly. They tied cords to each corner of the mat and lowered their friend through the roof to Jesus.

The people moved away to make room. They had never seen friends who cared that much!

Jesus looked up to the faces of the four men looking down from the roof. "You are full of faith", Jesus said. Then Jesus looked at the man lying on the mat. The people watching this surprising event could see that this man could not walk. But Jesus saw more than that. He saw that the man was sad because he had sinned. Jesus then said to him, "Your sins are forgiven. Get up at once. Roll up your mattress and walk home!"

The man believed Jesus and, even though he had not walked for many years he did as Jesus told him. His friends leaped from the roof, running after him.

Jesus could heal the man because He is God's Son and is all-powerful.

GUIDED PRAYER THOUGHT

> *Dear God, help us remember that you will always help us and that when we are sad or afraid we can talk to you and know that you will listen. We love you, God. Amen.*

BIBLE WORDS TO REMEMBER

> *Jesus said,*
> *"Those who are well have no need of a physician, but those who are sick do. But go and learn what this means: 'I desire mercy and not sacrifice.' For I did not come to call the righteous, but sinners to repentance."*
> Matthew 9:12

WORD MEANINGS

physician: _____

mercy: _____

sacrifice: _____

righteous: _____

sinners: _____

repentance: _____

QUESTIONS

1. What had the man in the story not been able to do? _____

   _____

2. How long had he been in this sad condition? _____

   _____

3. What did he do every day? _____

   _____

4. Where was he? _____

5. What sometimes happened?

   _____

6. What did his friends do?

   _____

7. What reasons were given in the story that told why?

   a. _____

   b. _____

8. Describe the town on one certain day.

   _____

9.　Did the man know where everyone had gone? _____

10.　How did this make him feel?_____

11.　What changed this feeling? _____

12.　What news did his friends hear about?

　　　_____

13.　What were his friends planning to do? _____

14.　The man could not walk. How did they get him to where
　　　Jesus was?_____

15.　What happened when they reached the house where Jesus was?

　　　_____

　　　_____

　　　_____

16.　Did the friends and the sick man know that they had a problem?

　　　_____

17.　Did they give up and go back home? _____

18.　What did they do? 　_____

　　　_____

19.　Why were the people in the house surprised?_____

　　　_____

20.　What did Jesus say to the four friends?_____

　　　_____

21. **What could Jesus see that the people could not see?**

_____

22. **What did Jesus say to the sick man?** _____

_____

23. **What two commands did He give the man?**

a. _____

b. _____

24. **What did the man do?** _____

25. **Why was it possible for Jesus to be able to make this man walk again?** _____

_____

Jesus had been talking to a large group of people as they sat on the shore near the boat He was in. He had been teaching them about God's love. They had listened for a long time. The sun was setting and it was getting dark.

Lake Galilee was very beautiful in the evening so Jesus and His disciples decided to go over to the other side of the lake. Since Jesus was very tired, He went to the back part of the ship to rest while the disciples rowed the boat.

While Jesus slept, all was not calm on the water. The disciples were not calm either! Suddenly there was a tremendous storm. The winds blew and the water splashed up on the boat. The disciples tried to row harder and soon became exhausted.

As the boat rocked, almost tipping over, the disciples became very frightened. But still Jesus did not wake up——He was sound asleep!

When the boat began filling up with water, they frantically shook Jesus awake. "Master! Wake up! Don't you care that we are all going to drown?"

Jesus was calm. He stood up in the little boat and rebuked the wind, and said to the sea, "PEACE, BE STILL."

At that moment, the wind stopped blowing and all was still and calm...except the disciples. They saw Jesus use His power and it was so awesome that they were frightened again.

Jesus looked at them and saw that they could not believe what they had just seen. They were confused—they wanted to believe but they were not sure that they knew who Jesus was and why He could do something that great.

"Why are you still frightened? Where is you faith in Me? Don't you know yet who I am?, Jesus asked.

The disciples seemed numb and afraid. "Who is this man?", they whispered to one another. "Even the wind and the sea obey Him!"

GUIDED PRAYER THOUGHT

Dear God, You are very great—-if even the wind and sea obey You, we should love and obey you even more because you love us so much. Help us find ways today to show you how much we love You too.   Amen.

BIBLE WORDS TO REMEMBER

Jesus arose and rebuked the wind, and said to the sea, "Peace, be still!" And the wind ceased and there was a great calm.
                    Mark 5:39

(Challenge)
Jesus said to His disciples, "Why are you so fear-ful?
How is it that you have no faith?" And they feared exceedingly, and said to one another, "Who can this be, that even the wind and the sea obey Him?"
                    Mark 5:40

WORD MEANINGS

shore: _____

exhausted: _____

frantically: _____

calm: _____

rebuked: _____

awesome: _____

relieved: _____

reaction: _____
_____

confused: _____

emotions: _____

numb: _____

obey: _____
_____

exceedingly: _____

QUESTIONS

1. Where were Jesus and His disciples? _____

2. What had Jesus been telling the people on the shore? _____
    _____

3. What time of the day was it? _____

4. Which lake (or sea) were they on? _____

5. Did Jesus suggest that they eat dinner?_____

6. What decision did the disciples and Jesus make?
    _____

7. How did Jesus feel after His day of teaching?

_____

8. What did Jesus do in the boat while the disciples were rowing?

_____

9. What happened while Jesus was asleep? _____

10. Could the disciples row the boat away from the storm? _____

11. Describe what was happening to the boat. _____

_____

12. How did the disciples react to what was happening?

_____

13. Did the wind and the waves splashing on the boat wake Jesus up?

_____

14. What made the disciples finally wake Jesus up?

_____

15. What did the disciples say to Jesus? _____

16. What question did they ask Jesus? _____

_____

17. What do you think they thought was going to happen?

_____

18. What was Jesus' reaction? _____

19. What did He do in regards to the wind? _____

20. What did He say to the waves? _____

21. What happened after Jesus spoke?

    _____

22. Were the disciples relieved? _____

23. Instead of responding in faith, how did the disciples feel?

    _____

24. What important question did Jesus ask?

    _____

25. What really impressed the disciples?

    _____

Things to think about:

1. How many emotions were expressed in this lesson? Name the
   ones you can find. _____

    _____

    _____

2. How do you think you would have felt if you had been one of
   the disciples and had seen the wind and the waves obey Jesus?

    _____

    _____

BIBLE FOUNDATIONS   LESSON 18

When Jesus and His disciples came again to the shore of the lake which was called the Sea of Galilee, people gathered all around Him. Many people had heard now about Jesus and that He could make sick people well.

One man was especially anxious. He was a ruler in the synagogue whose name was Jairus. He pushed his way through the crowds to come to Jesus. He knelt down before Jesus and said, "Please come to my house. My little girl is dying. Please! Come with me, Jesus, I beg you. Lay your hands on her so that she may be healed and live!

Jesus looked at the man's face which was full of anticipation and faith. "I will come with you", He said.

They started walking towards Jairus's house where his sick daughter lay. But the crowds were so great that they could not walk quickly. People were standing in the way . Then they saw another man hurrying through the crowd toward them. "Jairus! Jairus! It is too late. You do not need to bring Jesus now. Your little girl just died a few minutes ago."

Jesus heard what the man had told Jairus. The father looked so sad. He loved his little girl so much! But Jesus said to him, "Do not be afraid, only believe".

Then Jesus asked that no one follow Him except for a few disciples. They came to the house of Jairus where people were crying loudly and mourning the little girls death.

"Stop crying," Jesus said. "The girl is not dead, she is just sleeping."

The people that heard Jesus started laughing, thinking He did not believe that she had stopped breathing and was dead. "Doesn't He know when a person is really dead?" They were making fun of Jesus for not accepting the little girl's death.

Jesus told the people to leave the room where the girl was. He took her hand and said, "talitha cumi", which meant, "Little girl, it's time to wake up now!" The little girl awoke immediately. She looked up and stood up from her bed. She ran to her mother and father who hugged and kissed her, hardly believing their own eyes. Jesus had done what He said He would do!

As they tried to thank Jesus He said, "Get the little girl something to eat. I'm sure she must be very hungry after not eating for so long."

Jesus cares! The father believed that Jesus could make his little girl well and He did.

GUIDED PRAYER THOUGHT

Dear Heavenly Father, thank you for sending Jesus to show us your great love. We know that you care when we are hurt and sick. Help us to believe in You and have faith to know how much you love us. In Thy name We Pray, Amen.

BIBLE WORDS TO REMEMBER

Jesus said, "If you can believe, all things are possible to him who believes.
Mark 9:23

"The things which are impossible with men are possible with God."
Luke 10:27

"Assuredly, I say to you, if you have faith and do not doubt, whatever things you ask in prayer, believing, you will receive."
Matthew 21:21

WORD MEANINGS

anxious: _____

synagogue: _____

anticipation: _____

mourning: _____

assuredly: _____

request: _____

QUESTIONS

1. **Where were the people gathered in this story?**

   _____

2. **Which lake were they on the shore of?**

   _____

3. **Why did the people gather around Jesus?**

   _____

4. **What was different about one man who came to Jesus?**

   _____

5. What important position did this man have?

_____

6. What was the man's name? _____

7. Did the man get close to Jesus? _____

8. What did Jairus do when he got in front of Jesus?

_____

9. What was his request? _____

10. What reasons did he give for this request?

_____

11. What did Jairus want Jesus to do? _____

12. What did Jairus believe would happen if Jesus would do that?

_____

13. How did Jesus respond to the man's request?

_____

14. What prevented Jairus and Jesus from going to the sick girl quickly? _____

_____

15. Who came to Jairus and what news did he have? _____

_____

16. Did Jesus think it was too late to help her? _____

17. **What did Jesus say to Jairus?** _____

18. **How were the people acting when Jesus came to the house?**

    _____

19. **What did Jesus tell them?** _____

    _____

20. **Did the people believe what Jesus said?** _____

    _____

21. **What did Jesus tell the people to do?** _____

22. **What did Jesus say to the little girl?** _____

23. **What did the words He say mean?** _____

24. **When did the little girl wake up?** _____

25. **What did she do?** _____

26. **Were her parents surprised?** _____

27. **What did Jesus tell them to do?** _____

    _____

28. **Does Jesus always do what He says He will do?**

    _____

BIBLE STORY

After another day of teaching, Jesus and His disciples decided they would go away from the crowds to a quiet spot to rest. Jesus had so much to tell the people and He and His disciples had not even had time to eat a meal alone!

They got into their boat and rowed across the lake.

But the crowd had seen them and ran around the lake to meet Jesus on the other side. Even though Jesus was very tired and hungry, He had compassion for the people. He knew that they needed to hear how much God loved them. When He looked at them He thought tenderly of them as a shepherd who would care for his sheep. He thought, 'these people are like sheep with no shepherd to guide them'.

Jesus began to teach them and tell them how God wanted them to live so they would be content and happy and know how to please God. It became very late in the day and still the people stayed to listen to Jesus—-they were learning so much about God!

The disciples became a little impatient and said to Jesus, "Send these people away so that they can go into the villages and buy food—they need to eat.

Jesus said to them, "Give these people something to eat. They don't need to go into the town." The disciples were surprised that Jesus expected them to feed this crowd—-there were over five thousand people on that hillside! There was no way to do what Jesus told them to do. They did not have enough money to buy food for so many people.

Then Andrew, one of the disciples, brought a young boy to Jesus. "This little boy has brought food in his basket."

The boy opened up his basket for Jesus to see his lunch. "Take this food, Jesus," the boy said.

"Thank you," Jesus said, unwrapping the cloth. Inside the cloth were five small flat loaves of bread. There were also two small fish in the basket.

Andrew looked very doubtful, but it was all they had. "This will not feed all of these people," he said.

"Ask all the people to sit down in groups," Jesus told His disciples. Then Jesus held the bread for everyone to see. He thanked God for it and began passing it to His disciples to give to all the people.

From that one small lunch everybody ate and ate until they were full! And when they had eaten all they could, there was still enough food to fill twelve baskets!

Then Jesus sent the people to their homes so that He and the disciples could rest as they had planned. Jesus had performed a great miracle that day, but before He rested, He went into the hills to pray and talk to God.

GUIDED PRAYER THOUGHT

Thank you, Jesus for knowing just what we need. You had the power to multiply the small lunch so that there was enough for everyone. We know that You give us so many good gifts. Help us always to be thankful. Amen.

BIBLE WORDS TO REMEMBER

Jesus saw the people and was moved with compassion for them because they were like sheep not having a shepherd so He began to teach them many things.
Mark 6:34

Afterwards, Jesus departed to the mountain to pray.
Mark 6:46

Rejoice always, pray without ceasing, in everything give thanks; for this is the will of God in Christ Jesus for you.
I Thessalonians 5:16

WORD MEANINGS

1. compassion: _____
2. impatient: _____
3. doubtful: _____
4. performed: _____
5. miracle: _____
6. multiply: _____
7. need: _____
8. want: _____

QUESTIONS

1. What were Jesus and His disciples going to do?

    _____

2. Where would they go?

    _____

3. What were two reasons they wanted to do this?

    a. _____

    b. _____

4. How were they going to get to the other side of the lake?

    _____

5. Who saw Jesus and His disciples leaving to go across the lake?

    _____

6. What did the crowd do? _____

7. What emotion did Jesus have for the people? _____

8. What did the people need to know? _____

9. What did Jesus say the people were like?

    _____

10. How long did the people stay to listen to Jesus tell about God?

    _____

11. How did the disciples feel about the people staying so long?

    _____

12. **What did they say to Jesus?** _____

13. **Where did they want them to go?** _____

14. **Why did they want them to go there?** _____

15. **What was Jesus' response?—-What did He tell His disciples?**

    _____

    _____

16. **Why were the disciples surprised at what Jesus told them to do?**

    _____

    _____

17. **How many people were there to feed?** _____

18. **Which disciple found a boy with food?** _____

19. **What was in the boy's basket?** _____

20. **Was the boy willing to share his food?**

    _____

21. **Did the disciples think this would be enough to feed all these people?** _____

22. **What did Jesus tell the disciples to do next?**

    _____

23. **What three things did Jesus then do?**

    a. _____

    b. _____

    c. _____

24. Did everyone get enough to eat? _____

25. How much food was left?_____

26. What did Jesus do after the people left?

_____

Challenge Questions:

1. What did Jesus mean when He said that the people were like
   sheep without a shepherd?_____

   _____

2. Will Jesus meet every need we have? _____

   _____

   _____

3. What is the difference between a 'need' and a 'want'?

   _____

   _____

4. Name some of the things we need. _____

   _____

5. What are some things that you know are 'wants'?

   _____

   _____

6. What do we need to do so that we can stay close to God?

   a. _____

   b. _____

   c. _____

BIBLE FOUNDATIONS   LESSON 20

Every year, the Jewish people went to Jerusalem for a celebration called the "Passover". It was to remember the time God had helped the Israelites leave Egypt where they had been slaves, and God led them to a new land.

Jesus and His followers were also traveling toward Jerusalem. Before they reached the city, Jesus sent two of His disciples ahead. "Go into the next village. There will be a young donkey there that has never been ridden. Untie the donkey and bring it to Me. If someone asks you why you are taking it, tell them that the Lord needs it."

The disciples brought the little donkey to Jesus, happy that they could do something for HIM—-He was always doing things for them! They gladly laid their cloaks on the donkey's back so that Jesus could be more comfortable. The disciples were all smiling in anticipation. Jesus was going to Jerusalem—-they all wanted Him to be King!

Other people joined the disciples and followed as Jesus rode into the city. They kept chanting, "Hosanna! Hosanna! Sing praises to our King!

Parents and their children took fresh green branches from the palm trees and waved them as they marched and sang praises to Jesus. Other people put their palm branches down on the ground for the Jesus' donkey to walk on.

With all the shouting, the donkey became frightened, but Jesus was gentle as He patted and spoke kindly to the young animal.

Then people also laid their cloaks down on the road in front of Jesus, and everyone, those who ran on ahead and those who followed, joined in singing praises to Jesus.

"Praise God!
Blessings upon the Son of David
who comes in the name of the Lord!
Blessings upon the one who has come
to set up the kingdom of David.
Praise God! Hosanna! Hosanna!
His praises we sing!"

The singing became louder and louder as more people joined the crowd.

This was such an exciting day! But as they came close to Jerusalem, Jesus held out His arms towards the great city. Tears came to His eyes. He seemed all alone in the midst of the cheering and happy crowd.

"Oh, Jerusalem!", He said sadly. "If only you knew what I have come to do! I come in the name of the Lord, but I am not the kind of king you want right now, and I will not set up an earthly kingdom. You don't understand what real peace means!"

He was so grieved and sad for the people.

So Jesus entered Jerusalem with tears in His eyes. He loved these people so much, but they would soon turn their backs on Him and He would suffer for those He loved. He could not make them understand what He would have to do. He would die for the sins of ALL people so that, if they believed on Him, could live forever in heaven.

GUIDED PRAYER THOUGHT

> *We thank You God for sending Your Son Jesus. Help us to understand   how much you love us and accept Your gift. We know that we all have sinned and need your forgiveness. In Jesus Name, Amen.*

BIBLE WORDS TO REMEMBER

> *It is written:*
> *"There is none righteous, no, not one;*
> *there is none who understands;*
> *there is none who seeks after God.*
> *There is none who does good, no, not one."*
> *Romans:3:10-12*
>
> *BUT*
> *God so loved the world that He gave*
> *His only begotten Son, that whoever*
> *believes in Him should not perish but have*
> *everlasting life..*
> *John 3:16*

WORD MEANINGS

1. Jerusalem: _____
2. Passover: _____
   _____
3. Celebration: _____
   _____
4. Israelites: _____
   _____
5. Cloaks: _____
6. Chanting: _____
7. Palm branch: _____
8. Hosanna!: _____
9. Grieved: _____

QUESTIONS

1. **Where did the Jewish people go every year?**

    _____

2. **What was the celebration called?** _____

3. **What were they remembering?** _____

    _____

4. **Who was among all of those going to this great city?**

    _____

5. **What happened before they reached the city?**

    _____

6. **What did Jesus tell them they would find?**

    _____

7. **What instruction did Jesus give them?**

    _____

8. **What did Jesus say to do if someone tried to stop them?**

    _____

9. **Did the disciples do what Jesus asked?** _____

10. **What was the disciples attitude about helping Jesus?**

    _____

11. What did the disciples put on the donkey to make it comfortable for Jesus? _____

12. What did the disciples think was going to happen in Jerusalem?

_____

13. Who else followed Jesus into Jerusalem?

_____

14. What did the people chant?

_____

15. What did the children do? _____

16. What did they put on the ground? _____

17. Were the people afraid of being too noisy or did they just keep getting louder and louder in their singing? _____

_____

18. What did Jesus do as they came closer to Jerusalem?

_____

19. What tells us that Jesus had great emotion?

_____

20. What did Jesus say? _____

_____

21. What were the people looking for?

_____

22. What did Jesus say they did not understand?

_____

23. What would these people do who were now shouting "Hosanna!"?

_____

24. What was the reason Jesus had come?

_____

25. Why did Jesus choose to do this?

_____

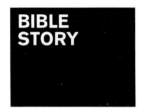

BIBLE STORY

A very special night had come for Jesus to be with His disciples and celebrate their Passover meal.

Jesus gave two of His disciples unusual instructions as He had when they had gone to get the donkey for Jesus to ride into Jerusalem.

"Go into the city", Jesus said. "A man carrying a water jar will meet you." The disciples waited expectantly for Jesus to continue. "Follow this man and when he comes to his house, ask the owner to show you the room where we will eat our Passover dinner. Then make everything ready for us."

The disciples did as Jesus told them. They were very excited about this special celebration night.

Evening came and Jesus, along with the other disciples arrived. Everything was ready. They took their places at the table quietly and began the Passover meal.

When they had eaten, Jesus got up from the table. He took off His outer robe and tied a towel around His waist. Then He poured water into a basin and began to wash the disciples' feet, and wipe them with the towel. As He came to Simon Peter, Peter said, "Lord, I can't let you wash my feet! That is a servants job. I should be washing your feet!"

Jesus answered him by saying, "What I am doing you do not understand right now, but one day you will understand." When Peter still protested, Jesus said, "If you do not let me wash your feet, you can no longer be My disciple." Then Peter said, "wash not only my feet, but also my hands and my head!" Peter felt so unworthy.

After Jesus had washed all of the disciples feet, He sat down and said to them, "Do you know what I have done to you? You call Me teacher and Lord and that is who I am. And if I will wash your feet, you should also wash each other's feet.

I did this to show you an example of how you should serve others. And the One sent with the message is not greater than the One who sent Him. Do not keep thinking about how important you are, but think of others. A servant is not greater than his master; you will be blessed if you know and remember these things.

Jesus suddenly looked very sad. He said,"I know that one of you will betray Me!"

The disciples became upset at Jesus' words. They kept saying, "Is it I, Lord? It would not be me, Lord!"

Jesus took the bread and broke off a piece and handed it to the disciple called Judas, and said to him, "Go quickly and do what you must!" Judas left the group and went out into the night——-he would betray Jesus that very night.

The disciples waited in anticipation for what Jesus would do. Jesus again took the bread. He thanked God for it, broke it and passed it to them. "This is My body, which is broken for you."

The bewildered disciples silently shared the bread. What did Jesus mean?, they wondered.

Then Jesus took the cup and passed it around to each of them. Again, He thanked God. "This stands for My blood. I will die so that others may live. When God made His first covenant with Moses, it was made with a lamb's blood. This is the New Covenant in which I will shed My blood. You will not see Me for a short time, but you will see Me again soon.

I am telling you this now before these events happen so that when the time comes, you will believe what I have told you. Those who believe who I am and why I came will live in God's kingdom forever.

The disciples still could not fully understand Jesus' words but they knew that something very important was going to happen soon.

GUIDED PRAYER THOUGHTS

Dear and Holy God, How much You must really love us to send Your very own Son who was willing to suffer and die so that we could live forever in heaven with You! Help us to love and serve each other as we love and serve You.   Amen.

BIBLE WORDS TO REMEMBER

A New Commandment I give to you, that you love one another; as I have loved you, that you also love one another. By this all will know that you are My disciples, if you have love for one another.

John 13:34

For God so loved the world that He gave His only son, that whoever believes in Him should not perish but have everlasting life.

John 3:16

WORD MEANINGS

1. **basin:** _____
2. **protest:** _____
3. **unworthy:** _____
4. **example:** _____
   _____
5. **blessed:** _____
6. **betray:** _____
7. **bewildered:** _____
8. **symbolized:** _____
9. **covenant:** _____
10. **suffer:** _____
11. **occur:** _____

QUESTIONS

1. **What special celebration was occurring?**

   _____

2. **Who was going to celebrate together with a meal?**

   _____

3. **What did Jesus give two of His disciples?**

   _____

4. **When had He done this before?** _____

   _____

5. **What four instructions did Jesus give them?**

   a. _____

   b. _____

   c. _____

   d. _____

6. **Did the disciples follow the instructions?**

   _____

7. **How did they feel about this celebration?**

   _____

8. **Were the disciples still preparing the room when Jesus and the other disciples arrived?**

   _____

   _____

9. Where did they sit? _____

10. What happened after they had eaten?

    _____

11. What two things did Jesus do first?

    a. _____

    b. _____

12. What were the next three things Jesus did?

    a. _____

    b. _____

    c. _____

13. What happened when Jesus came to Simon Peter?

    _____

14. What did Peter say?

    _____

15. Why didn't Peter want Jesus to wash his feet?

    _____

16. What did Peter say should happen?

    _____

17. Did Jesus think the disciples would understand why He was washing their feet?

    _____

18. Why did Peter say that He needed his hands and face washed also? _____

19. What did Jesus do after He had washed the disciples feet?

_____

20. Who did Jesus say that He was? _____

21. What reason did Jesus give for serving them?

_____

22. What did He say about being a servant?

_____

23. When would they be blessed?

_____

24. Why did Jesus look sad?

_____

25. Were the disciples surprised when Jesus said that one of them would betray Him? _____

_____

26. How did Jesus show which disciple it was?

_____

27. Which disciple would betray Him? _____

28. What did Jesus say to him?

_____

29. After Judas left, what did Jesus do with His other disciples?

_____

30. What was the New Covenant? _____

BIBLE STORY

The religious people who did not like Jesus' teaching were worried that He would be even more powerful than they were. They said, we must think of a plan to get rid of this man who says He is the Messiah, the one sent from God. "He even says He is God! He must be killed!

These people paid Judas, one of Jesus' disciples, so that he would betray Jesus. They arrested Him and He was brought to the rulers who would put Him on a cross to die.

Pilot, the Roman ruler in Jerusalem, could not find anything that Jesus had done wrong. But by then, the religious leaders had convinced the crowds that Jesus was not who He was. Pilot was afraid the people would riot if he released Jesus. When Pilot found Jesus innocent, the people shouted, "Kill Him! We and our children will be responsible for His death!"

Jesus, who had done things no other could do...He had healed people who were sick and made people alive who were dead. He had stopped the wind and waves during that stormy night when the disciples thought they would drown. Jesus said that God had sent Him and He had forgiven sins. When people believed He was sent from God, their lives changed—-they were happy, content and free.

They stopped doing the wrong things they had been doing and started pleasing God. They began to loved each other. They started caring for others instead of hating and lying and cheating. Jesus had never done anything wrong. He never sinned. He just showed the people how to love and kept telling them how much God loved them.

The people stopped listening now—He was on His way to die on a cruel cross. They hurt Jesus very much. But He still loved them. He loves all people everywhere. He loves you, too!

When Jesus was put on the cross, He looked sadly at those who had beat Him and spit on Him. He had the power to get down from the cross but He chose to die for the sins of the world—even you and me! God's plan was to send His Son as a sacrifice so that we could live forever in heaven with Him if we believe.

Jesus was not angry with the people who did not understand that he was the Son of God. He pitied them. He said, "Father, forgive them, because they do not know what they are doing." Those who were sorry for what they had done were forgiven. But there are consequences for doing wrong—just as there are for us. God's people and their children have suffered for rejecting Jesus.

This was a day of sorrow and sadness for those who loved Jesus. But there would be a glorious, happy day very soon!

GUIDED PRAYER THOUGHT

Thank you Jesus, for coming to earth to die for my sins and the sins of the world. No one could love us more than that! We know that You didn't have to die but You chose to do it so that we could some day live in heaven with you forever.
In Your Name we pray, Amen

BIBLE WORDS TO REMEMBER

> *For God so loved the world*
> *that He gave His only begotton Son,*
> *that whoever believes in Him*
> *should not perish but have everlasting life.*
> John 3:16
>
> *Jesus said, "My Father loves Me because I lay*
> *down My life that I may take it again. No one takes it from*
> *Me, but I lay it down of Myself, I have power to lay it down*
> *and I have power to take it again."*
> John 10:17

WORD MEANINGS

1. religious: _____
2. Messiah: _____
3. arrest: _____
4. released: _____
5. riot: _____
6. convinced: _____
7. Jesus' sacrifice: _____
8. crucified: _____
9. sorrow: _____
10. forgive: _____
11. consequences: _____
    _____
12. reject: _____
13. innocent: _____
14. responsible: _____
15. pity: _____
16. begotton Son: _____
17. perish: _____
18. eternal: _____

QUESTIONS

1. **Who was worried about Jesus' power?**

   _____

2. **What did they want to do?** _____

3. **What did Jesus say that made them so angry?**

   _____

   _____

4. **How did they want to get rid of Him?** _____

5. **Who did they pay money to betray Jesus?** _____

6. **Which Roman ruler said that Jesus had not done anything wrong?**

   _____

7. **Why did this man, who could have released Jesus, not do what the crowd wanted?** _____

8. **Name five things Jesus had done that are named in this lesson (there are many, many more!).**

   a. _____

   b. _____

   c. _____

   d. _____

   e. _____

9. How were people's lives changed?

    a. _____

    b. _____

    c. _____

    d. _____

    e. _____

10. Had Jesus ever done anything wrong or sinned?

    _____

11. What had He done that those who were trying to kill Him had seen?

    a. _____

    b. _____

12. What did the people do now? _____

13. What would happen to Jesus? _____

14. Did Jesus stop loving the people even though they wanted to hurt and kill Him? _____

15. Does Jesus just love the people who were on earth then?

    _____

16. Why didn't Jesus use His power to get down from the cross?

    _____

    _____

17. What does the bible say that people need to do to live in heaven forever? _____

18. What does the Bible say will not happen to those who accept and believe in Him? _____

19. Was Jesus angry with the people who did not understand who He was? _____

20. What did He ask God to do? _____

21. Why did He ask God to do that? _____
_____

22. Even though they were forgiven, did they suffer the consequences of their rejection? _____

23. How can we describe this day that Jesus died? _____

24. Is hope given for a brighter day? _____

BIBLE STORY

After Jesus had died, one of His followers, named Joseph, asked Pilot if he could take Jesus to bury Him in his own tomb.

The day after Jesus died and was buried was a day of remembering for those who loved Jesus. They tried to remember His words and understand why He had gone to the cross. The women prepared spices to take to the grave in an act of love.

Early Sunday morning, while it was still dark, the women walked the path to the tomb where Jesus was buried. Their hearts were very sad. "The stone in front of the tomb is much too heavy", one of the women said. "Maybe the gardener will help us move it."

Suddenly, the earth shook and there was a great brightness! As the women came closer to the tomb they saw that the stone was already rolled away and an angel stood before the tomb. His face was shining and his clothing was white as snow. The guards trembled in fear and fainted on the ground. The women were so frightened they could not move.

The angel said, "Do not be afraid, for I know that you are looking for Jesus who was crucified. He is not here; He is risen, just as He told you He would. Come inside and see the place where the Lord lay."

The women looked. The place was empty! The angel spoke again and said, "Go and tell His disciples that Jesus is risen from the dead. He will meet them in Galilee. Give them my message."

Quickly, the women left the tomb—-they had fear and great joy—-would the disciples believe what they would tell them? As they hurried back to the path, Jesus met them and said, "REJOICE!" They fell at His feet and worshiped Him. Jesus gently said to them, "Do not be afraid—Go to the others and tell them they will see Me soon."

What wonderful news! They couldn't wait to tell the disciples. They ran to the house where the disciples were and told them everything that had happened.

The disciples did not believe what the women said, and thought that they were just overcome with emotion. But it was puzzling, and Peter and John, wanting to be convinced the story was true, ran to see the grave themselves.

When they came to the tomb, they looked inside and found that it was true...Jesus was not there!

Later that day, two of the disciples were walking along the road, talking about what had happened and wondering what it could mean. Suddenly, Jesus joined them, but they didn't know it was Him. They invited Him to eat dinner with them.

When they finished their meal, He said to them, "Why are you so troubled? And why do you have many doubts?" They knew then that they had been with Jesus and that they had been talking and eating with their Lord and Master.

"Jesus!", they cried. "Why didn't we believe that He was really alive?", they asked each other. "We have seen the Lord for ourselves!"

Jesus said to them, "Peace be with you." Then they thought of what Jesus had told them many times, "Be at Peace. Don't be troubled or afraid. Always remember what I have told you—that I will go away, but I will come back to you again."

GUIDED PRAYER THOUGHT

Dear Heavenly Father,
Sometimes we forget Your words and become
afraid and confused when we have troubles.
Help us to have peace and remember how
much You love us—-and that You sent Your Son Jesus
who died for all the wrong things we have done and
now is alive in heaven.   In Your Name we pray,
Amen.

BIBLE WORDS TO REMEMBER

Jesus said, "Let not your heart be troubled;
you believe in God, believe also in Me.
John 14:1

I am the way, the truth, and the life.
No one comes to the Father except through Me."
John 14:6

WORD MEANINGS

1. joy: _____
2. tomb, sepulchre: _____
   _____
3. crucified: _____
4. risen: _____
5. rejoice: _____
6. overcome: _____
   _____
7. puzzled: _____
8. confused: _____
9. concern: _____
10. spices: _____
11. doubts: _____
12. confirm: _____

QUESTIONS

1. **What was the name of one of Jesus' followers in this story?**

   _____

2. **What request did he make to Pilot?**

   _____

3. **Where was Joseph going to bury Jesus?** _____

   _____

4. **What did Jesus' followers and disciples do after Jesus died?**

   _____

5. **Did they really understand yet why He had died on the cross?**

   _____

6. **What did the women do?** _____

   _____

7. **What was the reason they would do this?**

   _____

8. **When did they go to the grave?**

   _____

9. **How did the women feel as they walked along the path to the grave?** _____ _____

   _____

10. What were they concerned about? _____

_____

11. Who did they think might help them? _____

12. What happened when they approached the tomb?

_____

13. What did they see? _____

14. Who stood in front of the tomb? _____

15. What was his appearance? _____

16. What did his clothes look like? _____

17. What did the guards do? _____

18. How did the women react? _____

_____

19. What did the angel say? _____

20. Did the angel know why the women had come to the grave?

_____

21. What did the angel say that confirmed this?

_____

22. What wonderful words did the angel speak which changed
    everything the women thought?

    a. _____
    b. _____

23. What did the angel say that showed that they should have known this would happen? _____

24. What invitation did the angel give the women to prove what He had told them? _____

_____

25. Which word is past tense, meaning it was not true right now? _____

26. What did the women see when they entered the tomb?

_____

27. What three things did the angel tell the women to do?

a. _____
b. _____
c. _____

28. How did the women leave the tomb? _____

29. What two emotions did they feel as they left?

a. _____
b. _____

30. What did they wonder? _____

_____

31. Who did they see on the path? _____

32. What did He say? _____

_____

33. **What did the women do when they realized it was Jesus?**

_____

34. **What two things did Jesus tell them?**

    a. _____

    b. _____

35. **When the women told the disciples that Jesus was alive, did they believe?** _____

_____

36. **Which two disciples ran to see the grave?** _____

_____

37. **Did they find Jesus in the tomb?** _____

_____

38. **Later that day Jesus walked with two of his disciples. What two "why" questions did He ask them?**

    a. _____

    b. _____

39. **Did the disciples believe then?** _____

40. **What words did Jesus say to them?** _____

BIBLE STORY

Jesus spent forty more days with His disciples after He had risen from the grave. He reminded them of the important things He had taught them that they would need to remember after He returned to His Father in heaven.

"Peace I leave with you, My peace I give to you". Jesus said that this peace was not the kind of peace the world would give but would be a lasting peace that would not change.

Jesus had explained to them who He was this way: He said, "I am the true vine, and My Father is the vinedresser. You are the branches. Abide in Me, and I in you and you will bear much fruit; for without Me, you can do nothing.

As the Father loved me, I also have loved you; abide in my love.

If you keep My commandments, you will abide in My love, just as I have kept My Father's commandments and abide in His love."

Jesus said, "I am telling you these things so that My joy may remain in you, and that you may have abundant joy."

Jesus gave them a new commandment, just to love each other as He loved them. He told them that the greatest love is to lay down one's own life for his friends. Jesus said, "You are My friends if you keep My commandments." The disciples had listened carefully, trying to understand all of Jesus' words.

"You did not choose Me, but I chose you and appointed you so you could bear fruit and so that God will hear your prayers."

When Jesus was ready to ascend into heaven He reminded the disciples of their important work. "The whole world is ready and waiting for you to tell them the Good News," He said. "You must go and tell them that God sent His Son to die for all people everywhere. Go and teach them the things I have told you. Heal the sick, and make more disciples who want to tell others the Good News also. Teach others to obey all the commandments I have given you.

"And Remember! I am always with you, until the end of time.

Jesus promised that when He left them He would send His Holy Spirit to help them with the task He had given them to do. He told them to wait in Jerusalem together until this happened.

The disciples followed Jesus as He climbed the hills behind the village of Bethany.

While they watched, Jesus was taken up into heaven. They kept looking up, even though Jesus had disappeared into the clouds.

Two angels appeared and asked the disciples, "Why are you standing here looking into the heavens? This same Jesus will come back the same way you saw Him go some day.

GUIDED PRAYER THOUGHT

Dear God, help us to remember all the things Jesus taught and to keep Your commandments. Help us to love each other. Help us to tell others the Good News that You love them.
Amen.

BIBLE WORDS TO REMEMBER

Jesus said, Peace I leave with you, My peace I give to you; Not as the world gives do I give to you. Let not your heart be troubled, neither let it be afraid.
John 14:27

Jesus said, I am the vine, You are the branches, He who abides in Me and I in him, bears much fruit, For without Me you can do nothing.
John 15:5

Jesus said, I am with you always, even to the end of the age.
Matthew 28:20

WORD MEANINGS

1. vine: _____
2. vinedresser: _____
3. branches: _____
4. bear (fruit): _____
5. remain: _____
6. abide: _____
7. abundant: _____
8. commandments: _____
9. appoint: _____
10. ascend: _____

QUESTIONS

1. How many days did Jesus spend with His disciples after He was risen from the grave? _____

2. What did He remind them of? _____
   _____

3. Why was this time important for the disciples? _____
   _____

4. What did Jesus say He would leave with them? _____

5. How would they get this wonderful thing? _____
   _____

6. How was His peace different from the world's peace?
   _____

7. Jesus explained who He was to the disciples. To help them understand, He used an illustration:
   a. Who is the true vine? _____
   b. Who is the vinedresser? _____
   c. Who are the branches? _____

8. What did Jesus command His disciples to do? _____

9. What did He promise He would do? _____

10. What would result if they did what He commanded?
    _____

11. What will result if they did not do what He commanded?

_____

12. With whom does Jesus compare His love for His disciples?

_____

13. In whose love are the disciples to abide? _____

_____

14. What will result if we keep Jesus' commandments?

_____

15. Who has kept all of the Father's commandments? _____

16. What was the result? _____

_____

17. Why did Jesus tell these things? _____

_____

18. What did Jesus want His disciples to have? _____

_____

19. What new and important commandment did Jesus give His disciples? _____

20. What is the greatest love one can have? _____

_____

21. Who are we considered to be if we keep Jesus' commandments?

_____

22. Who chose the disciples? _____

_____

23. Who appointed the disciples? _____

24. What two reasons are given for why Jesus chose disciples?

    a. _____

    b. _____

25. What did Jesus remind the disciples of as He was ready to ascend into heaven?

    a. _____

    b. _____

26. What is the Good News? _____

_____

27. What are four things Jesus told His disciples to do?

    a. _____

    b. _____

    c. _____

    d. _____

28. What promise did Jesus give that is important to remember?

_____

29. How long will Jesus be with us? _____

30. Who would Jesus send to help His believers? _____

31. Where did Jesus go after He said these things? _____

32. What did the disciples do? _____

33. Who appeared? _____

34. What question did the angels ask the disciples? _____

    _____

35. What did they say would happen some day? _____

    _____

BIBLE FOUNDATIONS   LESSON 25

BIBLE STORY

Jesus promised the disciples that He would come back to earth again, and that when He returned from heaven EVERYONE would see Him.

The disciples had so many questions! Jesus had also told them that the temple in Jerusalem would not be left standing one day. The disciples did not understand—-the temple had been carefully built—-it was beautiful and strong—-how could its walls crumble?

So they asked Jesus, "When will these things be? And what signs will there be of your coming, and the end of the world?"

To help them understand, Jesus told a parable about ten young women who were going to meet the bridegroom and attend a wedding. With great anticipation, they went out in the night and took their lamps to wait for his arrival. Now five of the young women were wise, but five were foolish as you will find out as you hear this story.

The five wise young women had taken extra oil for their lamps, but the foolish women had taken none. When the bridegroom was delayed in his coming, they slumbered and slept. Their lamps grew dim and then went out.

Then at midnight, there was a loud cry and somebody called out—"The bridegroom is coming! Go out and meet him!"

The ten young women got up quickly to meet him, but only five had enough oil to light their lamps...the other five did not have oil to light their lamps and were not prepared to go to the wedding. They ran to buy more oil for their lamps while the five wise women went in to meet the bridegroom. When the other five came back, the door to the wedding was shut.

They shouted and said, "Lord, Lord, open the door!" But he answered and said, "I do not know you."

Jesus reminded the disciples that they should always be watching and ready for Him to come back, because no one will know the day or the hour when He will return.

He said that while those who loved Him waited for Him to come back, there would be people who would try to tell them wrong things about Him and try to persuade them not to believe in Him. Jesus said, "They will hate you and do bad things to you, but don't stop loving Me! I will take care of you and soon I will return with My angels with a great sound of a trumpet. Then I will take those who love Me to heaven to live with Me forever. "

"But those who have rejected Me and chosen not to love Me will be sent away to a terrible place and be separated from God forever."

**GUIDED
PRAYER
THOUGHT**

Dear Jesus, help us to be wise and obedient to Your Word. We want to be ready when you come back for us! Help us understand that You are in control and that all You do is for a purpose. As we wait, help us to remember that we need to tell others how much You love them so they will believe and love you, too.
Amen.

BIBLE WORDS TO REMEMBER

Jesus said, Heaven and Earth shall pass away, but My Words will not pass away.
Matthew 24:35

Watch therefore, for you do not know what hour your Lord is coming.
Matthew 24:42

He who endures to the end shall be saved.
Matthew 24:13

WORD MEANINGS

1. parable: _____

2. bridegroom: _____
   _____

3. slumbered: _____

4. persuade: _____
   _____

5. endures: _____

6. reject: _____

QUESTIONS

1. What did Jesus promise? _____
   _____

2. Will just the disciples see Him? _____

3. What did Jesus tell about the temple in Jerusalem?
   _____

4. **Why couldn't the disciples understand this?**

   _____ _____

5. **What two questions did the disciples ask about the end of the world?**

   a. _____

   b. _____

6. **How did Jesus explain this to them?** _____

7. **How many young women were there?** _____

8. **How many were wise?** _____

9. **How many were foolish?** _____

10. **Where were the women going?** _____

11. **What did they take with them?** _____

12. **What did they do while they were waiting?** _____

   _____

13. **What happened to their lamps?** _____

14. **What happened at midnight?** _____

15. **Who was Coming?** _____

16. **What were they going to do?** _____

17. What did they need to do before they could go in the dark?

_____

18. Which women had the oil for their lamps? _____

19. What did the five foolish women do? _____

20. Where did the five wise women go? _____

21. What had happened when the five foolish women came to the wedding? _____

22. What did the bridegroom say when they knocked on the door?

_____

23. From this parable, what was Jesus trying to help us understand?

_____

24. Does anyone know the day or the hour when He will come?

_____

25. What did Jesus say would happen to those who loved Him while they were waiting for Him?

        a. _____

        b. _____

        c. _____

        d. _____

26. What did Jesus tell us to do? _____

27. What did He promise He would do? _____

28. How would He return? _____

29. What instrument will we hear? _____

30. Where will He take the people who love Him? _____

31. What will happen to the people who have rejected Jesus?

_____

BIBLE STORY

The disciples were happy. They stayed in Jerusalem as Jesus had told them to do. They were full of joy and praise for their king, Jesus. They could understand now what Jesus had tried to tell them many times: "My kingdom is not on this earth, it is a heavenly kingdom, and some day all those who believe will be together in heaven, forever!"

The disciples and followers of Jesus couldn't wait to tell the whole world the Good News. They prayed and waited patiently together for the helper Jesus had promised to send. He had said, "I will send My Holy Spirit to comfort you and give you power to do God's work in the world."

Soon there were about one hundred and twenty people gathered in Jerusalem, people who had loved Jesus and wanted to follow Him. They believed that Jesus was the Son of God and they knew Jesus would send the gift He promised: The Holy Spirit.

There was another celebration in Jerusalem called "Pentecost" which is a Greek word meaning 'fifty days after the Passover'. This festival was important to the Jews because it was to remind them of the time when God gave the Law to Moses on Mount Sinai.

It was on this day of Pentecost that God sent His Holy Spirit to His disciples and followers. As the disciples prayed, God Himself swept through their midst and they were filled with joy and praise.

One said, "It was like a rushing, mighty wind!" Another described it as "being warmed and lit up by fire." The women, in awe of the experience said, "It was like the breath of God," and "like the coming of a dove."

The whole house was filled with the presence of God and each one felt the power within them. They suddenly were praising God together, but in many different languages. It was the Holy Spirit giving them words they did not understand but were a deep expression of praise to God.

As they were transformed by indescribable joy, they excitedly rushed into the streets of Jerusalem. They were no longer afraid of God and who He was because they knew that God's love had touched them in a very special way, giving them confidence and power to tell others the wonderful story of God's love.

All those who were there in Jerusalem who spoke different languages could understand what they were saying and they were amazed! " How could this be possible?", they asked. "What does it all mean?" Maybe these people have had too much wine to drink.. maybe they are just crazy!"

Peter talked to them and said, "God has brought Jesus back from the dead. We are witnesses to this. He has gone back to His Father in heaven but has sent His Holy Spirit so that we could tell you all this wonderful news. Please believe now and accept what is true.

Many people asked, "What do we need to do?"
Peter said, "Believe in Jesus, turn from your sins. Be baptized in the name of Jesus; then you will receive forgiveness and the gift of the Holy Spirit. This is God's promise to you."

GUIDED PRAYER THOUGHT

We thank You God for sending Jesus, now we can understand what Your love is really like. We thank You, too, for Your gift of the Holy Spirit who gives us confidence and power to do Your work here on earth. Amen.

BIBLE WORDS TO REMEMBER

Jesus said to His disciples: "Peace to you! As the Father has sent Me, I also send you."
John 20:21

"It is not for you to know times or seasons which the Father has put in His authority. But you shall receive power when the Holy Spirit has come upon you; and you shall be witnesses to Me in Jerusalem, and in all Judea and Samaria, and to the end of the earth."
Acts 1 7,8

WORD MEANINGS

kingdom: _____

Holy Spirit: _____

transformed: _____

indescribable: _____

language: _____

witnesses: _____

authority: _____

QUESTIONS

1. How were the disciples feeling? _____

2. Where did they stay? _____

3. Who were they praising? _____

4. What could they understand now that they had not understood
    before?_____

5. Where would believers be some day? _____

    _____

6. How long would they stay there? _____

    _____

7. What did the disciples want to do? _____

8. What did the disciples do while they were in Jerusalem?

    _____

9. Who were they waiting for? _____

10. What purpose did Jesus say this gift He was sending would
    have?_____

    _____

11. Other believers joined the disciples. How many people were
    gathered together in Jerusalem? _____

12. Why were these people gathered together? _____

_____

13. Who did they believe Jesus was? _____

14. What celebration was going on in Jerusalem? _____

15. What was this celebration for? _____

16. What happened on this day to Jesus' believers?

_____

17. How did they describe the coming of this promised gift?

    a. _____

    b. _____

    c. _____

    d. _____

18. How did this coming change the people who experienced it?

_____

19. What were the outward signs that resulted?

_____

20. Where did they go? _____

21. Were they afraid? _____

22. What did they do? _____

23. What did some of the people watching think about their strange
behavior? _____

_____

24. **What did Peter tell them?** _____

25. **What did Peter ask them to do?** _____

26. **When the people asked Peter what they should do, what did He tell them?**

    a. _____

    b. _____

    c. _____

    d. _____

27. **What would result?** _____

28. **What did Jesus say to His disciples in the book of John?**

_____

29. **Who had sent Jesus?** _____

30. **Who would Jesus send?** _____

_____

BIBLE STORY

A New story now begins. And yet it is still part of the Old story....the new part is that God's love has been revealed through Jesus. The old part is that God has ALWAYS loved His people from the very beginning of time. His love is endless and never changing. This story has gone on and on through the centuries. Many kinds of people have been part of this story.

The new part of the story begins in Jerusalem on one special day, but all the fascinating events unfolded from there spreading to every country in the world, even our own. It is a story that is happening right now, this very day, wherever we might be living.

You are part of it as we all are. Listen to the story.

It was all because of a man named Jesus. He came to earth as God. He lived as a human. That is very hard to understand but there was a special and important purpose. God had to show us what His love was really like. This is the only way He could show us how much He loved us.

Jesus loved everyone.
Jesus healed the sick.
Jesus fed the hungry.
Jesus taught people about God's love.
Jesus forgave sins.
Jesus never did anything wrong.
Jesus was perfect.
Jesus died.
Jesus went back to heaven.

But Jesus left behind power and He left behind love. The power was given to help people, not the kind in which the weak and helpless could be hurt.

This power came like fire
This power came like the winds
This power came like a dove.

It is the same power that God used when God made light out of darkness. It is the power that was there when Jesus told the wind and the waves to be still.
This power is still at work in the world.
It is the power of the Holy Spirit.
The love is the unchanging love of Jesus.
The people who believe in Jesus are given the love and the power.
They are the church of Jesus.

On that day when the power came to Jesus' disciples and followers in Jerusalem, three thousand people believed in Jesus! They wanted to be baptized and receive the Holy Spirit. All of these believers shared meals together. They prayed together and listened to the stories of Jesus. They met in the temple and worshiped God there.

Because they loved each other and were so kind to everyone, other people noticed that they were different and that they had peace in their lives. They wanted to know God in this way, too.

The church had been born and was growing.
But the church of Jesus is not a building.
The church of Jesus is not made of stone and wood or plaster.
The church of Jesus is all the people who follow Him, serve Him and obey Him.
The church of Jesus is people.
That is why the story has not ended.
That is why you and I are part of the story.

GUIDED PRAYER THOUGHT

Dear Heavenly Father, May we truly understand Your great love for us! Thank You for Jesus and thank You for sending the Holy Spirit into our lives so that we can feel Your presence. Help us to be kind to each other and show Your love to others so that they will accept Your love and be part of Your Church.
Amen.

BIBLE WORDS TO REMEMBER

"Let your conduct be without covetousness. Be content with such things as you have. Jesus said, "I will never leave you nor forsake you."
Hebrews 13:5

So we may boldly say: The Lord is my helper; I will not fear What can man do to me?
Hebrews 13:6

Jesus Christ is the same yesterday, today, and forever.
Hebrews 13:8

WORD MEANINGS

revealed: _____

centuries: _____

unfolded: _____

conduct: _____

covetousness: _____

content: _____

boldly: _____

existed: _____

QUESTIONS

1. **Why is this a new story?** _____

    _____

2. **What part of the story is old?** _____

3. **What is awesome and unique about God's love?**

    _____

4. **How long has this story existed?** _____

5. **Are just the Jewish people in this story?** _____

    _____

6. **Where did this part of the story begin?** _____

7. **When is this story happening?** _____

    _____

8. **Which people are part of this story?** _____

9. **Why do we even have a story to tell?** _____

10. **How did He come to earth?** _____

11. **How did He live on earth?** _____

12. **Why is that hard to understand?** _____

    _____

13. What was the purpose God had in sending Jesus?

_____

_____

14. What things did Jesus do to help people on earth?

a. _____

b. _____

c. _____

d. _____

e. _____

15. What didn't Jesus ever do? _____

16. What did He do that no earthly friend would do?

_____

17. When Jesus went back to heaven, what two things did He leave with us?

a. _____

b. _____

18. What was different about His power? _____

_____

19. Name the three ways His power came?

a. _____

b. _____

c. _____

20. When else was this power used?

a. _____

b. _____

21. Has this power stopped? _____

22. How is this power felt in the world today? _____

23. What kind of love is still with us? _____

24. Who is the church of Jesus? _____
_____

25. How many people believed in Jesus on the day Jesus' disciples and followers received the Holy Spirit in Jerusalem?
_____

26. From last week's lesson, can you remember what Peter told the people they must do to become a follower of Jesus?

    a. _____
    b. _____
    c. _____
    d. _____

27. What did the believers do?

    a. _____
    b. _____
    c. _____

28. What did they do at the temple? _____

29. What was their behavior?

    a. _____
    b. _____
    c. _____
    d. _____

30. **What was the result of their behavior?**

    a. _____

    b. _____

31. **What does not describe the church?**

    a. _____

    b. _____

32. **What three things do the people who are the Church of Jesus do?**

    a. _____

    b. _____

    c. _____

33. **How are you a part of the story?** _____

_____

_____

Don't let the story end for you! Tell others about God's love.

BIBLE STORY

Before His death, Jesus had said to His friends that He would be with them. When they realized that He was not dead but raised again, they were very happy and they understood why Jesus went back to heaven. They believed that He was with them to help them through the Holy Spirit, even though they could not see Him.

They believed that He was the Great King, the Messiah, and they wanted to tell everyone that Jesus was the One they had waited for so long. He was the One God had promised would come since sin entered the world in the Garden of Eden. Jesus was the One who could bring them peace and joy, they wanted everyone to know these wonderful things!

One morning, Peter and John were going to the temple in Jerusalem. Many people were coming to pray. At the door of the temple which was called the 'Beautiful Door', lay a beggar. He was not beautiful. He was so crippled that he could not walk at all. Every day, his friends brought him to this door, and he sat there all day and said to those who went in, "Give to the lame man, Please! Give to the lame man."

Peter said, "we don't have any money, but we will give you what we have. In the name of Jesus, walk!" Then Peter took hold of the man's outstretched hand and lifted him up.

The man felt that his feet and ankles had strength in them, and he stood and walked and leaped and loudly thanked God.

The crowd gathered and stared to see the lame beggar whom they had known so long. He was well and he was walking! Everyone was amazed.

The man pointed to Peter and John. "Here are the men who did it," he shouted. The people looked at Peter and John with looks of bewilderment.

Then Peter spoke.

"Do not stare at us", he said, "as if you think we did this in our own power. God gave Jesus to you, but your rulers would not hear Him, and killed Him; but God raised Him up again. Jesus healed this man. We worked in His name. He is still trying to show you God's love. He is calling you to let Him bless you."

The people who had wanted Jesus to die were upset. They did not want these followers to talk about Jesus. Many of Jesus' friends were arrested and put into prison for telling about Jesus.

But they did not stop loving Him! They told others in jail and even the prison guard became a believer. Jesus' followers were not afraid to let the whole world know that Jesus loved them and that God wanted them to believe and live in heaven forever with Him.

GUIDED PRAYER THOUGHT

Dear God, You have shown us your love in so many ways and You never give up on us! You even loved those who killed Your Son, Jesus. Help us to have courage to tell others about Your love and to show them Your love by living in the right way.
Amen.

**BIBLE
WORDS TO
REMEMBER**

*Jesus said, "I am the way, the truth and the life:
No man cometh unto the Father, but by Me."*
John 14:6

I can do all this things through Christ who strengthens Me.
Philippians 4:13

*All things work together for good to those who love God
and are called according to His purpose.*
Romans 8:28

QUESTIONS

1. **What had Jesus told His friends before His death?**

   _____

2. **How did they react when they realized that He was alive again?**

   _____

3. **When Jesus went back to heaven, why weren't they afraid?**

   _____

   _____

4. **Who did they believe He was?** _____

5. **What did they want to do?** _____

6. **How long had the people waited for this King Jesus to come?**

   _____

7. **What could Jesus do for people everywhere?**

   _____

8. Why didn't the disciples want to keep this Good News secret?

    a. _____

    b. _____

9. Where were Peter and John going one day? _____

10. Why were other people going there? _____

11. What was the door called by the temple? _____

12. Who was laying by the door? _____

_____

13. Who brought him to this door? _____

14. What did he ask the people who were going in the door?

_____

15. What did Peter say to the man? _____

16. What did Peter say he would give him? _____

17. What did he tell the man to do? _____

18. What did the man do? _____

_____

19. What did Peter do? _____

20. What did the man feel? _____

_____

21. **Then what four things did he do?**

     a. _____

     b. _____

     c. _____

     d. _____

22. **Who was watching?** _____

23. **Had they known this man for long?** _____

24. **What was their reaction?** _____

25. **What did the man say to them?** _____

26. **The people were** (check the ones that are true):

     a. **angry**   _____

     b. **happy**   _____

     c. **amazed**   _____

     d. **bewildered**   _____

27. **What did Peter not want the people to think?**

     _____

28. **Who did he tell them was the One who had the power to heal?**

     _____

29. **Did Peter remind the people of how they had treated Jesus?**

     _____

30. **How did Peter indicate that he and John were only helping Jesus?**

     _____

31. **What did Peter tell them Jesus was still trying to do?**

_____

32. **What else was Jesus doing through His followers?**

_____

33. **Were all the people glad to hear Peter's words?**

_____

34. **What happened to many of Jesus' friends?**

_____

35. **Did this stop them from telling about Jesus?**

_____

BIBLE STORY

Even though many people hated Jesus and tried to stop His followers from talking about Him, there were more and more who understood the meaning of God's love and why Jesus had come. They knew He was the One God had promised to send.

One man who hated Jesus and His followers was Saul. He said, "Kill them all. Don't let one of them remain alive!"

Saul was on the road to Damascus one day, planning to kill even more Christians. A great light dazzled him and he fell to the ground, blinded. A voice said,
"Saul, Saul, why are you persecuting Me?"
Saul cried, "who are You, Lord?"
"I am Jesus, the One you are persecuting."
Saul immediately answered, "Lord, what do you want me to do?"

God had chosen Saul for a very special and important work. Saul's eyes were healed and he no longer wanted to kill the Christians, he wanted to tell people everywhere about Jesus! He was totally changed and began using the name Paul.

Paul preached and wrote many wonderful letters to help Christians be strong and to have courage to believe God.

He wrote, "Don't tell lies to each other. You've thrown off your old self like old clothes, and you wear a new self, which God made and keeps working on from the inside of you so that you come to know Him better and better. Remember that your new clothes are love, kindness, peace and thankfulness."

When Christians were having problems and were discouraged, they could read Paul's letters. He said that no matter how difficult things were, Jesus would be with them. He said to "keep your eyes on the goal. Run the race with patience and Jesus will help you win and go to the finish line——Don't give up!"

Other apostles also wrote letters that helped believers then and help us right now know how God wants us to live with power and confidence.

James wrote, "Don't just listen to God's word, obey what God's word says. If you ignore His words, it is just like someone who looks in the mirror and sees a dirty face and messy hair, but then walks away and forgets to do something about it!"

"It is important to love people whether they are rich or poor. It does not matter to God how much money people have. He has a place for everyone in His kingdom."

"Be careful what you say! The tongue is very small but very powerful. Use it to say good things, not bad."

"Never forget to pray - God hears and answers prayer."

Peter also wrote letters telling Christians that they should always be kind and helpful to others so that "when they see your behavior, they will want to know Jesus, too."

"No matter what happens to you, you can know that Jesus will be back. Always be ready to meet Him and live everyday just like you thought today might be the day."

GUIDED PRAYER THOUGHT

Dear God, We know how much you love us. You have gone to a lot of trouble to tell us, and you are so patient with us! Help us to listen to Your Word and then obey it, never forgetting that You will be with us always to help us run the race. In Jesus Name,
                                        Amen.

BIBLE WORDS TO REMEMBER

If anyone is in Christ, he is a new creation; old things have passed away; all things have become new.
                        II Corinthians 5:17 I

Let us not grow weary while doing good, for in due season we shall reap if we do not lose heart. Therefore, as we have opportunity, let us do good to all.
                        Galatians 6:9-10

WORD MEANINGS

persecuted: _____

ministry: _____

weary: _____

due season: _____

QUESTIONS

1. **What did the people who hated Jesus try to do?**

    _____

2. **What was happening that made them even more upset?**

    _____

3. What did the people now believe? _____

_____

4. What was the name of one man who hated the Christians?

_____

5. What did He want to do? _____

6. Where was He going one day? _____

7. What was he going to do there? _____

8. What happened to him on the way? _____

9. Whose voice did he hear? _____

10. What did the voice say? _____

_____

11. How did Saul respond? _____

12. Do you think Saul already knew who was speaking to him?

_____

_____

_____

13. Did Jesus tell Saul who He was? _____

14. Did Jesus know all about what Saul had done and who he was?

_____

_____

15. **What question did Saul ask the Lord?** _____

_____

16. **What did God have planned for Saul?** _____

_____

17. **Who healed Saul's eyes so that he could see?** _____

18. **How did he feel different?** _____

19. **What did he want to do?** _____

20. **What was the name Saul began to use?** _____

21. **What ministry did Paul have?** _____

_____

22. **What did Paul tell them?** _____

23. **What did Paul say our old self is like?** _____

24. **How are we changed when we ask Jesus to be Lord of our life?**

_____

25. **What is our new self like?** _____

26. **Which four things does Paul mention as being a part of a**
    Christian's behavior?

      a. _____

      b. _____

      c. _____

      d. _____

27. What did Paul say we could do when we had problems?

_____

_____

28. How should we run the race? _____

29. Who will help us win and get to the finish line? _____

30. What did Paul say we should not do? _____

31. Which other apostles wrote letters to help believers know how God wanted them to live? _____

32. Give two things that James reminded Christians to do.

_____

33. If we don't do both of these, who did James say we are like?

_____

_____

34. What did James say about the tongue? _____

_____

35. What did he say about prayer? _____

_____

36. What did Peter write? _____

_____

37. What did he say the result would be if we had that behavior?

_____

38. **What did Peter say to remember when things were difficult?**

_____

39. **What should we be ready for?** _____

_____

40. **How should we live every day?** _____

_____

Challenge: **Write Galatians 6:9-10 in your own words. Tell what it means to you.**

BIBLE STORY

Jesus had told His disciples when He was with them, "I am going to heaven to prepare a place for you so that where I am, you will be too. In My Father's house are many mansions. If this were not true, I wouldn't be telling you. And I will come back for you."

John, the beloved disciple of Jesus was imprisoned on an island. While he was there, God showed him the things that would happen someday. John saw heaven in a vision, and saw the Lord sitting on a great throne with a scroll in His hands. This was called the Book of Life. When the scroll was opened, a great multitude of people from every land began singing praises to God. On the scroll were all the names of the people who believed in Jesus. Moms and dads, boys and girls, grandmas and grandpas and all those who love Him and have obeyed His commandments.

God told John to write about what he was seeing in this wonderful and glorious vision. It was so awesome that John wondered how he could find all the words to express what a wondrous sight this was!

John described the city as very bright, lit with the glory of God. Its gates are always open; for it is always daytime there. It will never be night again. Darkness and fear will be gone forever for those who love God and have been invited to that forever wedding feast. God invited EVERYONE but not everyone accepted the invitation.

There will be no tears or crying in heaven. No one will ever be sad again. There will be no death or loneliness. We will never again experience pain or sickness.

John saw all of heaven praising Jesus and worshipping God. John said he heard all of creation lift their voices: ALL creatures great and small gave Jesus praise and honor.

Then these words were written by John: "I, John who write this to you, heard and saw all these things. When the vision was gone, I knelt at the feet of the angel who had showed me these things."

The angel said, "It is God you must worship. I am just His servant. God's words must always be treasured."

Jesus said:
"I am coming quickly with a reward for you. I will give to everyone according to his work."
"I am the Alpha and the Omega, the Beginning and the End, the First and the Last."

Jesus will come back. He always keeps His promises!

GUIDED PRAYER THOUGHT

Dear Lord Jesus,
Thank You for Your words that tell of the wonderful place You are preparing for us. Thank You for planning all these beautiful things. Help us as we remember all of Your words and do what is right. And come back quickly, Jesus. We love You. Amen.

BIBLE WORDS TO REMEMBER

Jesus said, "I am coming quickly, and My reward is with Me, to give to everyone according to his work."

"I am the Alpha and the Omega, the Beginning and the End, the First and the Last."

Blessed are those who do His Commandments, that they may have the right to the tree of life, and may enter through the gates into the city.
Revelation 22:12-14

WORD MEANINGS

mansions: _____

imprisoned: _____

_____

vision: _____

scroll: _____

according: _____

rejected: _____

Alpha: _____

Omega: _____

QUESTIONS

1. **What had Jesus told His disciples when He was still with them?**

    _____

2. **Where was Jesus going?** _____

3. **What was His purpose in going?** _____

4. **What happened to John while he was imprisoned on an island?**

    _____

    _____

5.   What did John see in his vision? _____

6.   Where was the Lord sitting? _____

7.   What did He have in His hands? _____

8.   What happened when the scroll was opened? _____

9.   What was written on the scroll? _____

     _____

10. What did God tell John to write? _____

11. Do you think it would be difficult to express in words what he saw?
     Tell why. _____

     _____

12. Describe the city as John saw it.

     a.   _____
     b.   _____
     c.   _____
     d.   _____
     e.   _____

13. What will be absent from this wonderful and glorious heaven?

     a.   _____
     b.   _____
     c.   _____
     d.   _____
     e.   _____
     f.   _____

14. Who has been invited to come to the wedding feast (heaven)?

_____

15. Did everyone accept God's invitation?

_____

16. What else did John see? _____

17. What did he hear? _____

18. With what words did John confirm what he had written was true?

_____

19. What did John do when the vision was gone?

_____

20. What did the angel say? _____

_____

21. What did he say about God's words? _____

22. How did Jesus say He would come? _____

23. What did Jesus say He had for us? _____

24. Will everyone get the same reward? _____

25. Who did Jesus say He was?

    a. _____

    b. _____

    c. _____

26. What will Jesus do? _____

27. How do we know He will do it? _____

28. (Personal question) Is your name written on the scroll?

_____

What the Bible Says: Know

a. _____

b. _____

What the Bible Says: Do

a. _____

b. _____

c. _____

d. _____

What the Bible Says: Follow

a. _____

b. _____

c. _____

d. _____

Tell others about God's Love so that they will know Him too!

BIBLE FOUNDATIONS NEW TESTAMENT OVERVIEW

Evaluation/Response Card

We want to know how you liked it! Please take a moment to answer a few questions to help us evaluate the curriculum. To thank you for your time, we'll send you a coupon worth $2.00 towards your next purchase of any Explorer's curriculum workbook.

If you were to give this study a letter grade it would be: **A   B   C   D   F**

If there was one thing I could change about this course it would be: _____

_____

I found the lessons to be: a) too easy   b) about right   c) too hard

Age of student _____   Grade Level _____

Name _____

Address _____

City _____ ST _____ Zip _____

BIBLE FOUNDATIONS NEW TESTAMENT OVERVIEW

"And whatever you do, do it heartily, as to the Lord and not to men, knowing that from the Lord you will receive the reward of the inheritance; for you serve the Lord Christ."

1 Corinthians 3:23-24

We believe that good work should be rewarded! If you would like to receive an official *Certificate of Achievement,* please fill out this form and return it to us and we will send you a laser printed certificate suitable for framing with your name and the course you have completed.

Student's Name _____

Address _____

City/St/Zip _____

Phone # (___) _____

I certify that I have completed the *Bible Foundations New Testament Overview Course* to the best of my ability.

Signed _____

(Please enclose $1.50 to cover the cost of postage and handling. Allow 2-3 weeks for processing)

Explorer's Bible Study
P.O. Box 425
Dickson, TN 37056-0425